# HOT WORDS
## for the
# ACT ®

Linda Carnevale, M.A.

**BARRON'S**

*All inquiries should be addressed to:*
Barron's Educational Series, Inc.
250 Wireless Boulevard
Hauppauge, NY 11788
**www.barronseduc.com**

ISBN: 978-1-4380-0365-8
Library of Congress Control No.: 2014933716

Printed in the United States of America
9 8 7 6 5 4 3 2 1

**10%**
**POST-CONSUMER**
**WASTE**
Paper contains a minimum
of 10% post-consumer
waste (PCW). Paper used
in this book was derived
from certified, sustainable
forestlands.

# Contents

# PART III
# Reading Test: Humanities Vocabulary / 65

# PART IV
# Reading Test: Natural Science Vocabulary / 97

# PART V
# English Test Vocabulary / 129

# PART VI
# Writing Test Vocabulary / 161

# Introduction

## What role does vocabulary play on the ACT College Entrance Exam?

Sentence completion questions, like those on the PSAT and SAT, do not appear on the ACT exam. Knowing this, you might ask: What role does vocabulary play on the ACT College Entrance Exam? Vocabulary, in fact, plays a more significant role than you might initially think. Strong reading skills are important on all sub-sections of the test: English, Math, Reading, Science and, to an extent, even Writing. To perform well across the board and to earn a solid composite score, test takers need solid reading strategies and a broad and varied vocabulary. A steady level of concentration is very helpful as well; this is why it's both wise and worthwhile to take full-length practice tests when your schedule permits. By practicing you'll build up test-taking stamina and endurance in preparation for your actual test day.

The ACT Reading Test is comprised of four multi-paragraph passages. The passages come in four flavors: Prose Fiction, Humanities, Natural Science, and Social Science. To clearly and thoroughly absorb the information in these passages, it is beneficial for test takers to have a strong vocabulary. This is why *HOT WORDS for the ACT* features vocabulary lessons with words taken from all the above genres. This guide includes a broad and rich range of real ACT-type vocabulary taken from actual retired exams.

Use *HOT WORDS for the ACT* effectively, and you will broaden your knowledge of highly sophisticated words, in turn affording you a sharpened clarity about what you are reading. This will also help you answer more questions correctly and quickly. Most of the vocabulary in this book was pulled from actual Reading and English Test passages from retired ACT tests. The examples here are sure to give you an accurate sense of how challenging the test vocabulary will be for you.

---

### A Note About Our Choice of Hot Words

The words selected for this book are listed in the exact form and part of speech in which they appeared on real and retired ACTs. However, this book's approach is to mix things up and to illustrate the versatility and variation that characterizes real-life word use.

For example, *eclecticism* in its noun form is listed in Lesson 15; it is then used as an adjective, *eclectic*, in one of the illustrative sentences. Likewise, *sacrilegious,* an adjective, is listed in Lesson 7 and then used as a noun, *sacrilege*, in a sample sentence; and in Lesson 8, *mutual* is defined as an adjective and used in its adverb form, *mutually*, in one of the sentence examples. You may see any of these versions on the ACT you take.

These variations in usage will equip you with a broadened sense of how words can be used and tested. Remember that word forms are cut from the same cloth, so to speak. For example, *conformist* and *conformity* stem from the simple infinitive verb, *conform*. In Lesson 3 *concocted* is defined as a verb, but a sentence reflects its noun form, *concoction*. Similarly, *paradox* is listed as a noun in Lesson 12 and then used in both its adjective and adverb forms, *paradoxical* and *paradoxically*, in the sentence examples that follow.

---

## In which direction is the ACT moving in terms of vocabulary?

The 2012–2013 online ACT reveals that the Reading Test passages and their corresponding questions contain rich, varied, and upper-level vocabulary. Interestingly, the English Test—a test meant to assess ability on grammar, usage and mechanics, comprises five passages and also contains potentially challenging vocabulary.

My experience tutoring has taught me that vocabulary is often an obstacle for students on both of these verbal sections. Often, my ACT students will stop mid-passage (on the Reading *and* English Tests) and ask: "What does *prose* mean?" or "What does *attributed* mean?" Similar questions go on and on...

I always encourage my students, as I encourage you, to edify your test results by expanding your vocabulary. Learning more words will improve your ability to navigate the passages and their corresponding questions with greater ease and clarity of understanding.

## How much of the ACT content is based on English Language Arts?

All five subtests (English, Math, Science, Reading, and Writing) rely on your ability to read, think, and respond analytically. The math section, for example, features word problems, and the science test involves extended reasoning as well as a section on conflicting viewpoints of the passage authors. That said, this study guide focuses only on the three verbal portions (English, Reading, and Writing Tests) which are particularly heavy with vocabulary. It will be very beneficial for you to use this book to build a stronger and more diverse vocabulary—one that will aid you no matter what section of the test you are tackling. As you will discover as you work through this book, the English passages (which are made up of multiple-choice questions to test grammar, usage, sentence structure, syntax, and punctuation) contain potentially challenging words. To an even greater extent, the Reading passages tend to contain some hard words.

## What types of questions will I encounter on the ACT Reading Test?

Just as the flavors and topics vary from passage to passage, so do the types of questions you will be asked. Listed here, however, are the general question types you're likely to encounter. You may be asked to

- make generalizations as put forth by the author;
- draw conclusions about the author's expository method and organization;
- identify and interpret contrasts and comparisons;
- determine the main idea of the passage or a specific paragraph;
- formulate conclusions about the purpose of details or phrases as used by the author;
- determine the meaning of words and/or phrases as used in a particular context;
- interpret the author's tone, mood, or attitude pertaining to the topic.

## What are Test Takers' Anecdotes?

Test Takers' Anecdotes are firsthand examples of real situations that I have observed during tutoring sessions with my students. These anecdotes appear at the beginning of each lesson, and they illustrate concretely how vocabulary can be an obstacle to a student's success when answering questions on the English or Reading Test. These real-life examples demonstrate how a student with a stronger and broader vocabulary will be in a better position to answer a greater number of questions correctly.

## What are Memory Tips?

Memory Tips are the mnemonic aids provided at the end of each lesson. These tips feature a variety of methods for learning and retaining vocabulary words. These methods include focusing on root words, prefixes, synonyms, common usage, chants, associations to preexisting knowledge, and visual cues. You may want to keep a notebook in which you rewrite these tips and even create new ones of your own. You'll find these mnemonic aids very effective in solidifying your comprehension of new words.

For easy reference, at the end of this book, you will find a section called **Memory Tips Reviewed**. This is a consolidated list of all tips contained within *Hot Words for the ACT*. Go ahead and interact with this list to customize it to your own particular needs. Highlight tips in color to indicate which words you know and which require further study. Underline word roots and prefixes. Use the section as a mini workbook, where you highlight, mark, underline, doodle visual aids, and add tips of your own.

## What is the Purpose of the Review Exercises?

A series of review exercises follow the Memory Tips. These exercises include two types: Matching, and Words in Context. These exercises include questions you would not encounter on the real ACT; rather, they are designed as a vocabulary self-test for you. The exercises will help you gauge how much you've learned and help you to reinforce your vocabulary as you revisit the words again.

# Part I
# Reading Test:
# Prose Fiction Vocabulary

Questions in this category of passages are based on complete short stories or excerpts from short stories, novels, novellas, memoirs, or other works of fiction.

## Word Bank

The words below are from the Prose Fiction section of ACT practice exams. These words have all presented some level of difficulty, confusion, or uncertainty for students. This comprehensive list includes words from the passages themselves, from the questions, and from the answer choices. Not every word in this vocabulary bank is included in the following lessons, which feature only ten words each. Only those words that tend to appear most frequently on exams or those that students found the most unclear are examined in depth.

## Prose Fiction Reading Passages

Words listed appear within the passages and/or their corresponding questions. **Test 1**: accustomed, adapted, ample, aristocratic, arrogant, bristled, embittered, frailness, gaudy, grazing, gilt, illusions, inferred, prose, resemblance, scrutinizing; **Test 2**: accommodate, acrid, ambiguity, apathy, brimmed, calamity, camouflaged, carcasses, commonplace, conventional, decipher, disdainful, exacting, extravagance, feign, improvisation, indifference, inevitably, inferred, irrevocably, gestures, grumbled, meander, meticulously, momentous, nostalgia, primordial, prose, protracted, summon, unison, vendors, vivid, voluptuous, vulnerability;

**Test 3**: accessible, accommodate, adapted, arbor, attributes, brace, brooder, communion, concocted, disheartens, dismantling, introspective, involuntarily, kindling, lush, meticulous, prose, remnant, remote, reverently, self-contained, serenity, skeptical, traits, vividly; **Test 4**: absentminded, accorded, array, askance, bedrock, brash, breadth, collective, conferred, cue, deliberate, dissonance, hokey, languid, lyricism, maelstrom, profane, prose, speculated; **Test 5**: affect, anxiously, bandanna, broadcasts, consumes, discontent, fluctuations, grim, heap, kettle, monitors, penned, prairies, prose, ranchers, scorch, soberly, sulky, tinged

# Lesson 1

## Test Takers' Anecdotes

While reading a Prose Fiction passage about dreams, Leah found herself confused about the narrator's description of the dream because she thought **amniotic** (pertaining to a fluid-filled embryonic sac) had to do with atoms and cell structure instead of water. Certainly, a more expansive vocabulary would have been a great asset to Leah.

On this same Prose Fiction passage, adapted from a short story titled "The Threshold," Peter found himself distracted by the use of the word **threshold**. Peter said he had never heard this word before and he truly had no reference for it. Because the word was used several times, it obviously clouded his understanding of much of the reading. Immediately, in the opening paragraph, the word appeared: "She stays at the **threshold**, and the door is always closed, refusing her entrance." Later the word distracted Peter again and again: "She is like a tired traveler who stops at the **threshold** and stays there, stationary as a plant... She is a traveler on a long trip, who stops at the **threshold**, half dead with fatigue...." If Peter had known at the outset that **threshold** pertains to a doorstep or an entrance to a new place or dimension, he would have felt at ease.

Throughout the passage, Peter found himself faced with a number of other words that, although not very difficult, were still a bit outside his comfort zone: **revelation, stationary, console, superficial, accustomed, latter, trivializing**, and **rational**. Later, among the questions, several words presented a challenge for him: **despairing, detached, resigned, dismayed, amniotic, whim, rationality**, and **essence**. For example, here's one question that gave him some trouble:

As it is used in line 58, the word **humor** most nearly means:

**A.** personality.    **B.** whim.    **C.** mood.    **D.** comedy.

At first, Peter was tempted to pick *comedy* as he felt it was most closely related to *humor*. But rereading the word in context made it clear to him that this did not make sense. Then he wanted to pick *whim*; as this was an unknown word for him, he thought it was the answer. Eventually he gleaned from context that *humor* was best defined as the woman's personality: "She thinks I have a power that she doesn't have and this brings out her envy and bad *humor*."

> **accustomed, adapted, aristocratic, bristled, embittered
> frailness, gaudy, grazing, inferred, prose**

---

**accustomed** (adj.)   adapted to present and existing conditions; used or practiced regularly, often; adapted to particular conditions, habits, or customs

> The nutritionist advises that we feed our bodies so they become more **accustomed** to whole foods, fruits, lean meats, and vegetables rather than processed foods.

> **Accustomed** to a lifestyle in which she plans her daily agenda, Daniella would find it exceedingly difficult to return to work full time.

> The mergers and acquisitions lawyer is **accustomed** to eight hours of sleep. Pulling two all-nighters and watching the sunrise from his office window drained him for days.

**adapted** (v.)   made new or made to fit appropriately, often through revision or modification; made suitable to a particular situation; modified; tailored

> The literary excerpt was **adapted** from the original, longer work of fiction by English novelist Charles Dickens.

> The critically acclaimed off-Broadway production was **adapted** from a popular post–World War II novel.

> As a junior year transfer student, Susie has **adapted** seamlessly to the research-based university.

**aristocratic** (adj.)   characteristic of or having the qualities of a privileged class; elitist; of or pertaining to nobles; socially high-ranking and exclusive

> Owning the finest things that money can buy does not make the woman, despite her **aristocratic**, yet superficial, air of superiority.

With five-star dining and world travel, the couple's lavish lifestyle, combined with their elegant though affected manner, seemed **aristocratic**.

Toting her latest designer bag and fashion-forward shoes, she comes across as more than **aristocratic**; she is downright snobbish!

**bristled** (v.)   to have raised bristles, as in aggression, fear or anger [**bristle** (n.) refers to a short, stiff, coarse piece of hair.]; to demonstrate an intensely defensive attitude, as in response to another's criticism or hurtful comment

Feeling indignant and defensive, Shelly **bristled** at the accusations of greed and manipulation that were directed toward her.

The audience was fully engrossed and amused, for the high school theater production **bristled** with dry humor and private jokes that, unexpectedly and delightfully, the majority of the audience seemed to get!

About to embark on a new career, Norman was excited to begin this revitalizing chapter in his life **bristling** with possibilities.

**embittered** (adj.)   feeling bitter or aggravated; characterized by feeling a sense of acrimony, rancor; hateful or aggrieved

Though she encountered unfairness, hard knocks, and disappointment, Beshma is an indomitable optimist who refuses to feel **embittered**.

Disappointed by the self-centeredness of the people around him, Carson became increasingly **embittered** by the shallow and self-consumed nature of his acquaintances.

Feeling **embittered** about the injustices she witnesses, Lara religiously practices Zen breathing as a means of dispelling negative energy through cleansing breaths: long deep inhales, hold, slow exhales.

**frailness** (n.)   physical weakness; inability to carry out strenuous activities; easily destroyed or broken; fragileness; unsubstantial

> His physique conveyed a sense of **frailness**; the form of his body appeared to lack adequate nutrition, protein, and exercise.

> The **frailness** of her voice does not allow her to command much authority or power over those in her social circle who are more assertive and vociferous.

> Although Gavin has an incredible level of stamina, the **frailness** of his lanky frame erroneously convinced the swim instructors that he shouldn't pass the lifeguarding pre-test.

**gaudy** (adj.)   garish, offensively extravagant, or distasteful; ostentatious in a tasteless and showy way; tawdry; outlandish

> The **gaudy**, heavily-frosted purple eye shadow cheapened the dancer's appearance.

> Extremely **gaudy** earrings made it hard for Hilde's listeners to take her opinions seriously because they were overly focused on the "bling-bling" of her large hoops!

> Jake's Manhattan loft was appointed with **gaudy** furnishings and accessories: zebra stripes, garish gilt, and neon blue leather.

**grazing** (v.)   lightly touching or rubbing up against something in passing by; eating small, light portions of food throughout the day

> The kindergartener **grazed** his knee on the brick exterior of the house as he searched behind the hedges for his tennis ball.

> Intent on trimming her caloric intake, Nina was **grazing** on sliced carrots, celery, and mushrooms dipped in salsa from morning until night.

> Trying to get his attention, she would intentionally **graze** his arms and shoulders as she reached for the notebooks on his desk.

**inferred** (v.)   derived as a conclusion from facts or underlying assumptions; reasoned from evidence and premises; implied; surmised

> **Inferred** conclusions are those that evolve from "reading between the lines."

> Winona observes couples living apart and **infers** a weak marriage; seeing geographical distance, she erroneously **infers** emotional distance.

> Your calm, lighthearted appearance leads us to **infer** that you feel secure and content.

**prose** (n.)   a literary medium, such as a long or short work of fiction, memoir, or essay; language that resembles ordinary writing and speaking; all writing except for poetry

> Henry is a prolific **prose** writer; he has written five novels, three novellas, and seventeen short stories.

> To polish one's **prose**—eliminating errors in grammar, usage and mechanics—a writer should engage in the rigorous, recursive process of editing and revising.

> "I am a poet, not a **prose** writer," Billy the bard flatly asserted.

---

## MEMORY TIPS

Use these mnemonics (memory devices) to boost your vocabulary. Make up your own memory clues for words in this lesson that are personally challenging. Add these tips, and your own, to your Vocabulary Notebook.

### ac<u>custom</u>ed
To connect to this vocabulary word, focus in on the basic word built into it: *custom*. Just as a custom is an aspect of life that people are used to, so **accustomed** means feeling familiar with or habituated to something or someone.

### bristled

Picture the *bristles* of a hairbrush. They are pointy, coarse, and sharp to the touch. Connect these tangible feelings to the emotions behind the verb **bristled**: bitterness, coarseness, sometimes even fear.

### embittered

Focus on the basic word built into this word: *bitter*. Knowledge of this stem word will help you remember the meaning of *embittered*: "feeling bitter, resentful, or disillusioned."

### frailness

Think *frail*. Now link *frail* to a mental picture of a thin, rickety, wooden *rail* that is ramshackle, unsteady, and about to fall down. This visual mnemonic device will help you to remember that frail pertains to people or things that are weak, unsteady, or debilitated to some extent or another.

---

## MATCHING

Match the vocabulary words in Column A with their defining characteristics in Column B.

**Column A**

1. aristocratic
2. infer
3. bristled
4. frailness
5. embittered

**Column B**

A. weakness or fragility

B. feeling sour, resentful, rancorous

C. pertaining to an elite or noble class, to the ranks of lords

D. to deduce or conclude through the use of reasoning

E. verbally retaliated in a tone of offense

F. tastelessly showy or overdone; ostentatious

G. writing other than poetry

## WORDS IN CONTEXT

Based on the context in which each **bold** word is used, identify the word usage of each sentence as either C (Correct) or I (Incorrect).

1. Although he is normally upbeat and chipper, Jeremy spoke with an **embittered** tone of voice that led his friends to believe he was feeling down and disillusioned.

2. **Inferring** the author's meaning as a protest against urbanization, Xavier decided to make this personal perspective the theme of his term paper.

3. Following a ten-week course in etiquette training, their **aristocratic** mannerisms became second nature.

4. Despite the **frailness** in her bone-thin arms and legs, the patient unwisely avoided the use of weights, ignored her body's need for increased protein, and refused calcium supplements.

5. So angry that she saw fire-engine red, Lydia **bristled** in response to their off-base criticisms and accusations.

# Lesson 2

## Test Takers' Anecdotes

Mike had some degree of trouble connecting with the narrator's perspective, upon reading these lines in paragraph three of the short story: "I am awake, keeping my **vigil** over the Midwest's **pastoral** kingdom." Later, Mike wasn't perfectly certain about this final reading question: "According to the passage, news reports **attributed** the cosmonaut's knees buckling to..." He didn't fully comprehend the meaning of *attributed*.

Samantha read a Prose Fiction passage adapted from the novel, *The Antelope Wife*, by Louise Erdich. She enjoyed the story line and it held her attention, so she had little difficulty absorbing the passage and answering its corresponding set of ten multiple-choice questions. Nonetheless, she did take the initiative to create flashcards with these words encountered in the first of the two columns of the passage: **sage**, **cobalt**, **weary**, **muffled**, and **beckons**. Eager to learn as many new words as she could, Samantha also wrote down the meanings of **discreet** and **maneuvering**, which appeared on a Prose Fiction passage excerpted from a short story based on Latino-American history.

---

**conventional, exacting, feign, gestures, meander, primordial
protracted, unison, voluptuous, vulnerability**

---

**conventional** (adj.)  based on established beliefs, practices; trite; tending to be more conservative than adventurous; traditional; customary

> **Conventional** thinkers are unlikely to consider and imagine alternatives outside the box of their mental status quo.

> Roast turkey, sweet potatoes, and stuffing are essential parts of a **conventional** Thanksgiving meal.

> Yogic breathing, manipulation of the muscle-skeletal system, and daily meditation are not central to most **conventional** allopathic medical practices and therapies.

**exacting** (adj.)  characterized by requiring keen concentration, diligence, and stringent attention to detail; rigorous; strenuous; demanding; challenging

> **Exacting** standards are required to gain acceptance into the more competitive joint-degree programs that fast track your education.

> An **exacting** yoga practice includes deep-seated lunges, side stretch sequences, and seated twists.

> An **exacting** cook, Tamara uses only the freshest, organic meats and seasonal produce in her savory and exotic meal preparations.

**feign** (v.)  to fake; to put on a false appearance of; to pretend; to represent falsely

> Lacking even an iota of curiosity about college basketball, Sheila **feigned** interest in March Madness, so she could spend time cozying up with her boyfriend on the couch while eating chicken wings and nachos.

> An astute doctor can detect when his hypochondriac patient is either **feigning** symptoms or genuinely feeling ill.

> Uncle Louie would **feign** weak hearing; he would tell Aunt Gertrude that he didn't hear her tell him to stop at the supermarket, fix the leaky faucet, or take out the garbage.

**gestures** (n.)  bodily movements (usually of the limbs) that are expressive in nature; something done or spoken as a kindness, formality, or courtesy, for its effect on others

> The exaggerated **gestures** of the Broadway actors in *The Book of Mormon* were sometimes startling; other times, dramatic and comical.

> Commanding the attention of every bus driver, parent driver, and student pedestrian, the theatrical crossing guard stationed between the middle school and high school used a repertoire of arm and hand **gestures** like no other!

> As the party was quieting down and clearing out, Lia whispered to Dylan, "**Gesture** to me when you're ready to leave."

**meander** (v.)   to move through or stroll along a course or path in a winding, indirect, or sinuous fashion; to wander aimlessly; to ramble

> Shopping for silver and turquoise sunflower pendants, Chris and Linda **meandered** through the maze-like aisles of vendors at the Mexican Arts and Crafts Market.

> **Meandering** along the curving shoreline that extended for miles, the boys hardly realized how far they had walked beyond the Hacienda del Mar resort property.

> As they leisurely **meandered** through Central Park on an April afternoon, the family took a ride on the merry-go-round, shopped the souvenir vendors, and climbed the bedrock.

**primordial** (adj.)   relating to that which was first developed or created; in existence from the beginning or earliest of times; primitive, elemental, fundamental; primeval

> Mother's **primordial** instincts took over when she chased after the schoolyard bully to give him a piece of her mind.

> The ravenous teenage boys eyed the skewers of juicy barbecued meats with a **primordial** intensity much like that of tigers glaring at their prey.

> Touring a downtrodden, residential area of St. Thomas allowed the vacationers to understand the **primordial** living conditions of some of the Caribbean island natives.

**protracted** (adj.)   extended in duration; prolonged in space or time; lengthened

> Although the baseball practice was called from three to five o'clock, it was **protracted** to six thirty in the evening.

> **Protracted** by an hour, the caddie training session ended at one o'clock instead of at noon.

> Relishing every hour of their tropical vacation, the family decided to **protract** their stay from one week to ten days.

**unison** (adj.)   identical in musical pitch; harmonious union or agreement; accord, unanimity

> In **unison**, the vivacious kindergarteners bellowed, "I scream, you scream, we all scream for ice-cream!"

> "Happy New Year!" was loudly shouted in **unison** by more than fifty convivial guests at the festive New Year's Eve party.

> Side by side, swimming in **unison**, the ladies did thirty-three laps in the forty-foot-long pool.

**voluptuous** (adj.)   characterized by pleasure and luxury; pertaining to the attractiveness of an individual's body

> With its bright orange ripened flesh and sweet nectar taste, the papaya is one of the world's most **voluptuous** fruits.

> The **voluptuous** white marble sculpture and fountain are focal points in the Italian square.

> Bestowed with **voluptuous** curves, the radiant model beautifully filled out the fully-beaded designer gown.

**vulnerability** (n.)   capability of being emotionally hurt; sensitivity; the state of being open to emotional wounds

> To avoid showing her **vulnerability** to others, Jeanne put up a tough front and kept her guard up at all times.

> His kindness and gentle nature sometimes leave him **vulnerable** to the hurtful conduct of others.

> To avoid being **vulnerable** to the insensitivity and selfishness of others, edify yourself by engaging in positive habits, investing time in your health, and behaving with good will toward everyone.

## MEMORY TIPS

Use these mnemonics (memory devices) to boost your vocabulary. Make up your own memory clues for words in this lesson that are personally challenging. Add these tips, and your own, to your Vocabulary Notebook.

### primordial
Split this word into two parts: *prim* and *ord*. Expand these parts to create the phrase, "primitive order." Creatively cutting a word into its parts is a great way to recall and harness its meaning.

### unison
The prefix *uni-* means "one" or "singular." Consider this prefix as it is used in *unilateral, universal, unicorn, unicycle,* and *unicellular.* When people are singing in *unison*, they are singing as if they share **one** voice.

## MATCHING

Match the vocabulary words in Column A with their defining characteristics in Column B.

**Column A**

1. vulnerability
2. feign
3. protracted
4. unison
5. voluptuous

**Column B**

A. extended in duration

B. full and curvy in physical body

C. capacity for one's feelings to be hurt or one's physical body to be harmed

D. primitive, from the earliest of times

E. to pretend or fake

F. all together as one

G. to move or travel in a winding fashion

## WORDS IN CONTEXT

Based on the context in which each **bold** word is used, identify the word usage of each sentence as either C (Correct) or I (Incorrect).

1. The sisters **protracted** their beach vacation from ten days to one week.

2. **Feigning** a green thumb, Uncle Andrew appointed his house with plastic but life-like green plants and ferns.

3. Adorably, the affectionate husband **gestures**, with wide-open arms, for his wife to cuddle up next to him on the family room couch.

4. Flat and crispy, toasted pita rounds are a **voluptuous** type of bread.

5. Brown rice sushi is not a **conventional** food served at baseball and football stadiums.

# Lesson 3

## Test Takers' Anecdotes

Seth was confused by a question that appeared on a Prose Fiction reading passage because he did not understand the meaning of the verb, *attributes*. The question stated: According to the passage, Ted *attributes* which of the following characteristics to the redwoods?" Seth expressed that he ended up guessing because he couldn't wrap his head around what the question was asking. As an action verbal, **attributes** means "assigns the cause of something to somebody, or assigns qualities to someone or something."

---

**accessible, arbor, concocted, disheartens, dismantling
introspective, involuntarily, lush, remnant, serenity**

---

**accessible** (adj.)   capable of being reached; state of being within reach; easy and pleasant to deal with and communicate with; capable of being influenced; capable of being accessed, seen, or utilized; available for use

> Both malls are easily **accessible** by the express bus that leaves the campus's centrally located Student Union.

> To the pre-med student, physics and chemistry are not only **accessible**, but also intellectually intriguing.

> Securing the steering wheel with a hefty, red metal LoJack device, Filippo made his car less **accessible** to thieves.

**arbor** (n.)   most typically built of wooden lattice or metal work, an arch-shaped structure covered with branches or climbing vines, often used for ornamental or shelter purposes in a garden

> Delicate pink clematis climbed up one side of the **arbor**, draped across the top, and made its way down the opposite side to the ground.

> The trumpet flower vines mingle with the grape vines of the metal lattice **arbor** that shades their backyard patio.

> The gate at the bottom of the metal **arbor** opened to the slate patio on which a fire pit and chairs were situated invitingly.

**concocted** (v.)   put together, made, or prepared by combining various materials, elements, or ingredients; fabricated, created, or devised, as in a plan

> Using a heart-healthy mix of oats, bananas, berries, flaxseed, walnuts, fat-free milk, and organic honey, she **concocted** a large pan of baked oatmeal that provided warm, nutritious breakfasts for the week.

> Far handier than most men, Sandy **concocted** an air-tight attic door using remnant wood, plastic stripping, and miscellaneous hardware and hinges he found lying around the utility room.

> Anger is a complicated emotion. According to modern day psychology, it is a **concoction** of several intense emotions including fear, desperation, and insecurity.

**disheartens** (v.)   causes someone to lose his or her spirit or sense of morale; discourages; dissuades

> An unfavorable interview **disheartens** the young executive in his job search.

> "Do not be **disheartened** by one low grade," the teacher pleaded. "You can turn your average around by working hard during the weeks ahead."

> Even though Sofia strives to maintain an optimistic, healthy attitude, the negativity of those around her sometimes **disheartens** her spirit.

**dismantling** (v.)   tearing down, taking apart so that the whole system or piece of equipment, for example, no longer functions as a whole

> **Dismantling** the interior and exterior holiday decorations was a family-wide effort.

> When the sports stadium was completed, it was time to **dismantle** the scaffolding and cranes.

> Alex's summer job involved **dismantling** indoor equipment (like horses, hurdle walls, mini trampolines, and a temporary rock climbing wall) which was used at the summer camp for obstacle courses.

**introspective** (adj.)   looking inward to examine one's feelings, thoughts, and ambitions; self-examining; reflective

> To determine what factors in life will truly make you happy, devote some **introspective** hours getting to know who you are and what will make you feel fulfilled.

> Both worthwhile uses of our time, soul-searching and **introspection** go hand in hand.

> **Introspectively**, vividly imagine your future on a day-to-day level. How would you like to spend your time? This **introspective** activity can help you choose a suitable career path.

**involuntarily** (adv.)   done against one's will; not subject to one's self control or autonomy

> Because of financial struggles, Frank was **involuntarily** forced to take a job across the country from his family.

> Tragically, the character in the tear-jerker movie was **involuntarily** committed to a home for the mentally impaired.

> **Involuntarily**, we digest and absorb our food without giving this complex metabolic process much thought.

**remnant** (n.)   a relatively small, leftover part; a trace remaining of something; in commerce, an unused or unsold good

At the Pottery Barn factory store, **remnants** go on sale next month.

**Remnants** of her decade-long dance career, her pink ballet slippers and shiny tap shoes decorated the shelves of her basement dance studio.

To economize, the Bensons purchased a **remnant** piece of carpet for their spare bedroom.

**serenity** (n.)   an emotional state in which an individual is free from stress, worry, or disturbance; an untroubled state of mind; ease, calmness, tranquility, peacefulness

Striving for a sense of **serenity** in her home, which she has nicknamed the "Zen Zone," Leah often lights ivory candles, diffuses lilac-scented oils, and encourages her family to keep television volumes low.

Nothing is as perfect as a sunny day at an ocean beach to fill us with **serenity** and wash our cares away.

**Serenity** and contention are polar opposites; where there is strife, there is no peace.

**lush** (adj.)   growing abundantly, especially rich young growth; green, verdant, flourishing, thriving; luxurious, particularly with regard to furnishings and decoration; opulent, lavish

A **lush** expanse of palm trees graced the entrance to the tropical resort.

The golf caddies enjoyed the peaceful feeling of spending a few hours on the **lush** green of the perfectly manicured golf course.

Known for his green thumb, Ernie toiled contentedly in his **lush** vegetable garden that rimmed with broccoli heads, tomato plants, and sprawling cucumber vines.

## MEMORY TIPS

Use these mnemonics (memory devices) to boost your vocabulary. Make up your own memory clues for words in this lesson that are personally challenging. Add these tips, and your own, to your Vocabulary Notebook.

### concoct
Consider the prefix *con-* (*con-* means "with, together") in words such as *concordance, congregate, convene*, and *connect*. Also, let concoct and combine connect in your mind as viable synonyms. Both have two syllables and start with *co-*, which is another prefix meaning "together."

### disheartens
The prefix *dis-* has a negative, reversing force. Depending on the word in which it appears, *dis-* can also mean "away from" or "against." Recall the use of *dis-* in these words: *disallow, disembark, disappear, disbelieving, dislike, disagree, disapprove, disregard*, and so forth. If someone **disheartens** your dream of starting a business, he or she "works against" or "takes away" your ambitious, entrepreneurial heart or spirit.

### introspective
Split this word into two parts: *intro* and *spect*. As a prefix, *intro-* means "within" and "inwardly." As a root word, *spect* has to do with seeing, as in in*spect*, *spect*acles, *spect*ator, and circum*spect*. Breaking down a word into its parts is a great way to remember its meaning.

### lush
Visualize in your mind's eye a supersized bright green "lush bush." Actively picture this **lush** bush brimming with large, green healthy leaves! Recite this tongue-twisting chant to secure this word's meaning: "Lush bush! Lush bush! Lush bush!"

# MATCHING

Match the vocabulary words in Column A with their defining characteristics in Column B.

**Column A**

1. remnant
2. concocted
3. arbor
4. serenity
5. accessible

**Column B**

A. looking inward to examine one's life and purpose; self-examining

B. full of robust, green growth

C. created, devised; imaginatively conceived

D. available for use; able to be reached or accessed

E. a leftover portion or piece; remainder

F. peacefulness, tranquility

G. a wood lattice structure that may serve as an arch-shaped decoration or covering in a garden

# WORDS IN CONTEXT

Based on the context in which each **bold** word is used, identify the word usage of each sentence as either C (Correct) or I (Incorrect).

1. **Involuntarily**, I made a point to send the happy couple an engagement card and gift.
2. The harmonic sound of cascading water created an atmosphere of **serenity**.
3. To keep the sprawling lawn looking **lush**, give it plenty of seed, water, and fertilizer.
4. With a bent toward science and math, Jordan found the course "Romantic British Poetry" to be rather **inaccessible**.
5. Self-obsessed individuals are typically more **introspective** rather than genuinely concerned about others.

# Lesson 4

## Test Takers' Anecdotes

The word **speculated** appeared in a Prose passage excerpted from a novel about a musician: "It had to do, she **speculated**, ...with the way he held his head, angled to the left like that, tilted toward both heaven and earth." Not only was Tina unable to define the word, but she also had trouble answering the multiple-choice question relating to that precise part of the passage. Once I defined the word for Tina, she reread that part of the passage and was able to answer the question correctly. In this contextual usage, **speculated** means "mulled something over in terms of its various possibilities, conjectured, wondered." Notice again how a strong and broad vocabulary can help a student perform better on the Reading Test.

> **absentminded, accorded, array, askance, breadth**
> **cue, dissonance, languid, profane, speculate**

**absentminded** (adj.)   having the tendency of being forgetful, preoccupied, inattentive, mentally scattered; distracted

> Distracted and **absentminded**, the pre-teen athlete headed to his soccer game without wearing his shin guards or team jersey.

> To combat her **absentmindedness**, the overextended woman tried eating more fish (brain food), taking her daily multivitamin, and getting adequate sleep.

> The ***Absentminded*** Professor is the title of a 1961 Walt Disney Production film.

**accorded** (v.)   to give to someone or something, in alignment with what is or has been earned, appropriate, or due

As scholar-athletes, Varsity players are **accorded** particular campus privileges such as ninth period free!

On account of her kind and self-effacing nature, selfless Sheila was often **accorded** special courtesies and exceptions to stringent rules.

The college-bound senior was **accorded** several scholarships based on his community service and volunteer efforts.

**array** (n.)   a large assortment, variety; a big number; an order or regular arrangement of people, things, ideas, items

The **array** of fresh fish available at the outdoor grill was incredible: salmon, tuna, shrimp, among others.

The beach vendors offered an **array** of items for sale, including sundresses, beaded necklaces, and hand-painted wooden bowls.

Troy's **array** of interests was expansive and included math research, public speaking, baseball, and fine foods.

**askance** (adj.)   with a sideways look or glance; obliquely; with an expression of distrust or disapproval; contemptuously

Homeowners Leanne and Jim eyed the backyard intruder **askance**.

Glaring **askance** and seething, Gia made her boyfriend nearly tremble with an intensely scornful look that said, "You are in the doghouse!"

With an **askance** glance, Hilary made her skepticism clear.

**breadth** (n.)   a quality of comprehensiveness; scope; vastness, expansiveness; width

At the young age of five, the **breadth** of Chester's travels include San Juan, Cabo San Lucas, Rome, Miami, and Italy's Adriatic Coast.

Despite the **breadth** of her undergraduate and graduate school studies, she remained aloof to the inequities that exist among men.

"Describe the **breadth** of your volunteer experiences," the community-minded interviewer inquired.

**cue** (n.)   a signal or indication (as a word, phrase, or bit of stage business) to a performer to begin a specific speech or action; something serving a similar purpose; a hint

> Following a swift wave of Ms. Ajel's hand, on **cue**, the kindergarteners sat on the reading carpet and chanted, "Criss-Cross Applesauce!"

> Heeding his mother's nonverbal **cues**, the respectful teenager offered his grandparents glasses of ice water and sat next to them for a chat.

> Taking a visual hand **cue** from his baseball coach, the batter bunted.

**dissonance** (n.)   lack of harmony or agreement; strife; discord

> A peacemaker, Lia religiously avoids **dissonance** in all areas of her life.

> An atmosphere of dissent and **dissonance** can engender nervousness and ill-will among the parties involved.

> Assonance and **dissonance** are viable antonyms.

**languid** (adj.)   draining of energy from exhaustion; listless; weak; sluggish in personality and energy level; slow moving; exhibiting a lack of energy or enthusiasm

> On humid, hazy summer afternoons, nothing enlivens a **languid** spirit quite like an invigorating dip in a crisp, cool pool.

> **Languid** Lenny, upon receiving four free concert tickets to see his favorite band, had nothing much to say except for a quiet, expressionless "cool" and "thanks."

> After giving an hour-long tour in 95-degree heat, the university tour guide **languidly** strolled to the student union to find shade and a refreshing frozen yogurt.

**profane** (adj.)   vulgar; irreverent; unconcerned with religion or that which is considered sacred

Unlike the melodic and spirit-lifting music played at the yoga studio, the dance club blasted tunes that were unnerving and **profane**.

The parents were disgusted by the **profane** language used by teenagers in Facebook and Twitter posts.

The **profane** actions of individuals tell us who they really are; their words can mask their true essence.

**speculate** (v.)   to wonder, to guess, to put forth an opinion; to ponder over; to conjecture

Given her son's proclivity for science and interest in health, she **speculated** that he would make a fine radiologist or anesthesiologist.

Given that Panera Bread is one of Jodi's favorite places for lunch, her parents **speculated** that they might bump into her when they stopped there for a bite to eat.

Equipped with a high-precision telescope, Bob gazed at the celestial universe and **speculated** about abstract concepts such as black holes, dwarf stars, and time warps.

## MEMORY TIPS

Use these mnemonics (memory devices) to boost your vocabulary. Make up your own memory clues for words in this lesson that are personally challenging. Add these tips, and your own, to your Vocabulary Notebook.

### array

Rhyming clues can be particularly effective. *Array* and *display* rhyme. Let these sentences, which incorporate *array* and *display*, help you solidify this word's definition. Remember, an **array** is a large collection or group of things that relate to each other...

The jewelry party hostess will now *display* an eye-catching *array* of bedazzled earrings.

Jack is happy to *display* his *array* of sports collectibles and baseball caps.

Excited to *display* his *array* of Italian desserts, the pastry chef assembles a Viennese table brimming with cannoli, éclairs, and rainbow cookies.

### <u>bread</u>th

Ciabatta rolls, French baguettes, Italian bread, challah, rye, wheat, pumpernickel, sourdough....Think about the expansive variety of bread there is in the world. Now let *bread*, found in *bread*th, remind you that **breadth** pertains to the far-reaching range of something.

### <u>dis</u>sonance

The prefix *dis-* means "against" or "without." Consider this prefix in words such as *disconnected, disagreement, discouraged,* and *disjointed*. *Sonic* means pertaining to sound. Recall how dolphins use sonic communication to call to and locate one another in the water. Put the word parts together and you get something like "against sound," another way of saying "without harmony."

## MATCHING

Match the vocabulary words in Column A with their defining characteristics in Column B.

| Column A | Column B |
|---|---|
| 1. languid | A. lack of agreement; strife |
| 2. absentminded | B. an expansive assortment; a large number or a wide range of items or people |
| 3. breadth | |
| 4. askance | C. a signal or indication, usually to start something |
| 5. array | D. preoccupied, distracted, forgetful |
| | E. a range, measurable width or extent of something |
| | F. lacking energy, lifeless; lethargic |
| | G. sideways glance; slanted |

## WORDS IN CONTEXT

Based on the context in which each **bold** word is used, identify the word usage of each sentence as either C (Correct) or I (Incorrect).

1. Avoiding eye contact, cold-as-ice Ursula looked **askance** at her rival, Gwen.

2. Her expansive and expensive **array** of designer shoes and handbags included some made by Gucci, Prada, and Fendi.

3. A brisk, forty-minute walk outdoors rejuvenated him, lifting that heavy, **languid** feeling.

4. Acknowledging his companion skier's **cue**, Harrison followed her lead, detouring off the beginner green slopes and onto the blue intermediate trails.

5. What has been the **breadth** of your overseas travel?

# Lesson 5

## Test Takers' Anecdotes

The word **penned** presented confusion to several students who encountered it in a Prose Fiction passage set in the northern prairies of Montana. **Penned** was provided as an answer choice for a word-in-context question. One student, a varsity wrestler, associated this word with *pinned*, and so he did not pick it. Another student associated this same word with the past tense of writing. She, too, did not pick **penned** as the answer. Turns out, the correct answer was **penned**, a viable synonym, in the given context, for *fenced*: "I washed some cucumbers...in the water. Then I fenced them in with my hand and poured off the water into the kettle on the stove."

---

**affect, consumes, discontent, fluctuations, grim
heap, monitors, penned, sulky, tinged**

---

**affect** (v.)   to create a change; to have an influence over; to act upon in a manner that produces a response, outcome, or change

> Allergies to shellfish **affect** her ability to enjoy a spectacular waterside, seafood dinner.

> Lemon water with a touch of natural cranberry juice can positively **affect** the health of your digestive system.

> If you train your mind to think positively and constructively, then negative conditions created by outside forces should not adversely **affect** your well-being.

**consumes** (v.)   to destroy completely; to squander, spend lavishly; to use up; to drink or eat in large quantity; to fully engross or absorb

An obsession that **consumes** most of her free time, shopping is the central focus of Cassie's existence.

**Consumed** by her appearance, Uma wears only the latest trends in clothing, jewelry, and all fashion accessories.

Mindful of healthy eating, Adrienne **consumes** a great deal of grilled fish, fresh fruits, and lightly steamed vegetables.

**discontent** (n.)   a lack of contentment or a restless desire for things to get better; dissatisfaction; unhappiness, ill at ease

Feeling **discontent**, Dennis seeks to deflate the full and happy hearts of those in his midst.

Gabriel suffered from **discontent** when his parents would not support his passion for music and concert going.

Bella felt **discontent** when she received her disappointing report card.

**fluctuations** (n.)   changes, variations, ups and downs with relation to degree, level, and value; waverings

Miranda must be under a great deal of stress, as her mood **fluctuations** range from calm to irritable.

Extreme **fluctuations** in the weather caused Gia to wear Uggs one day and flip-flops the next!

The price of home heating oil **fluctuates** daily.

**grim** (adj.)   gloomy, somber, sullen; stern in manner or appearance

As she has never held a regular job, her prospects for gaining steady employment are **grim**.

*Grim Prairie Tales* is a 1990 American horror film composed of four tales and set in the Midwest.

The coach's face looked **grim**; we knew the news he had to share with us would not be good.

**monitor** (v.)   to watch, keep track of, or check, usually for a special purpose

> Nurses constantly **monitored** the patient's heart rate.

> An effective business continually **monitors** and responds to client concerns and suggestions.

> A control freak, Cal religiously **monitors** every hour of his family's social calendar.

**penned** (adj.)   shut in or closed up in what is, or what feels like, a somewhat small place of confinement (especially pertaining to animals)

> **Penned** indoors for weeks due to household responsibilities, Tina was overjoyed to finally spend the day at the shopping mall.

> The Jack Russell Terrier and Labrador mix were **penned** in a large, metal crate positioned in a shady corner of the backyard.

> Using a couple of long planks of wood, the homeowners **penned** the turtles into a makeshift cage and situated the enclosure alongside the bluestone patio.

**sulky** (adj.)   gloomy, sullen, moodily silent

> Even though they devoted the entire day to spending time together, Willa could not help but feel that Dario was in a **sulky** mood: he barely spoke and exhibited no energy at all.

> **Sulky** Susan could use lessons in positive thinking. Her gloomy demeanor makes us feel that she holds the weight of the world on her shoulders.

> Nicknamed "Sad Sack," Nick personifies **sulkiness**: he wears a forlorn and defeated expression from dawn to dusk.

**tinged** (v.)   colored with a slight stain of color or shade; tinted; affected with a subtle taste or smell; a delicate suffusing of color or hue; an influence; an affecting touch

> Jake's gloating was **tinged** with a sincere sense of sadness for his friends who didn't receive as great news as he had.

> Mrs. Jenkin responded to the development with a feeling of exaltation, moderately **tinged** with apprehension.

> Their relationship was **tinged** with rancor and an unhealthy vibe of competition.

---

## MEMORY TIPS

Use these mnemonics (memory devices) to boost your vocabulary. Make up your own memory clues for words in this lesson that are personally challenging. Add these tips, and your own, to your Vocabulary Notebook.

### discontent
*Dis-* is a negative-indicating prefix. Depending on the word in which it appears, *dis-* can mean "against" or "not." Consider this prefix as used in *disavow, disrespect, disagree, disrepair,* and *disappear*. So, individuals who are **discontent** are *not* feeling content, satisfied, or happy.

### penned
If a wrestler is "pinned down" on the mat in one of his fighting matches then, in a sense, his opponent has our wrestler "confined or controlled," which is a solid definition for **penned**. Again, to make new vocabulary words your own, creatively link familiar and similar sounding words to your new vocabulary words.

### tinged
If one's actions leave one feeling "tinged with guilt," then these emotions are, in a sense, tinted (colored, painted) with guilt. Tinted windows on a sports car are highlighted or aesthetically touched up with a smoky gray shade. **Tinged** and *tinted* look and sound similar, so you can use your familiarity with *tinted* to connect you to the meaning of **tinged**.

## MATCHING

Match the vocabulary words in Column A with their defining characteristics in Column B.

**Column A**

1. sulky
2. consumes
3. penned
4. affect
5. monitors

**Column B**

A. to have an influence on; to create a change on something or someone

B. has a great hold over one's time and interests

C. melancholy; somber and gloomy

D. assesses the progress of; oversees a process or situation

E. corralled, trapped; held down

F. colored, touched, painted with a hint of something

G. has a great hold over one's time and interests

## WORDS IN CONTEXT

Based on the context in which each **bold** word is used, identify the word usage of each sentence as either C (Correct) or I (Incorrect).

1. A diehard "fashionista," Fiona finds that tracking the latest trends **consumes** a great number of her waking hours.

2. A self-confessed "hover-mother," Jane closely **monitors** the activities of her children's days.

3. **Sulky** Sally surprised us all with a warm, genuine smile!

4. Snow and ice kept the elderly man **penned** indoors for days.

5. The science fiction movie was enhanced by staggering special **affects**.

# Part II
# Reading Test:
# Social Science Vocabulary

Topics addressed in this category of passages include anthropology, archaeology, biography, business, economics, education, geography, history, political science, psychology, and sociology.

## Word Bank

The words in Part II are from the Social Science section of ACT practice exams. These have all presented some level of difficulty, confusion, or uncertainty for students. This comprehensive list includes words from the passages themselves, from the questions, and from the answer choices. Not every word in this vocabulary bank is included in the following lessons, which feature only ten words each. Only those words that tend to appear most frequently on exams or those that students found the most unclear are examined in depth.

## Social Science Reading Passages

Words listed appear within the passages and/or their corresponding questions and answer choices. **Test 1**: bureaucrats, circumscribed, concede, deterred, diligent, electorate, eloquent, frankly, indifference, inertia, intricacies, judiciary, layman, legitimacy, orator, perquisites, populace, regulations, tirade; **Test 2**: abstract, alleged, ambiguously, articulated, credulity, creed, disavows, dispel, eloquence, eloquent, embalm, foresaw, harbingers, ideological, imminent, ingeniously, inquiry, irony, oracle, prophet, prophetic, quasi, rebuke, sacrilege, sacrilegious, seminal, sentiments, spawned, treason, veil; **Test 3**: bequeaths, durable, elaborate, emissions, innovation, innovative, linear, mutual, onus, prototype, revel, streamlined; **Test 4**: allocate, appalling, barren, bias, constitute, corroding, detached, fringe, grim, infrastructure, inordinate, integrated, mandate, municipalities, obliterating, objective, revitalize, riddled, sluggishly, spurred, urban, utility; **Test 5**: acoustics, amphitheaters, archaeology, aspirations, attributes, contempt, courtiers, depict, doctoral, erroneous, façade, feigned, flaw, hemmed, inaccessible, intact, integrity, marvel, notable, obscuring, ravages, simulation, spectators, tableau, testament, unaffected, ushered, ventilated, virtually, yields.

# Lesson 6

## Test Takers' Anecdotes

Grant missed a Social Science reading question because he felt the vocabulary in the question-and-answer choices was, in his words, "really tough." These words and phrases included: **alleged**, **notion**, **sacrilegious**, and **strains credulity**. We proceeded to make flash cards to eliminate any confusion next time he encountered these words—whether on this test or in his everyday life and schooling, in conversation, or in his required reading for school.

In a Social Science passage about rain forests and sustainability, Olivia felt frustrated because she didn't know the meaning of **fledgling**, as used in the multiple-choice reading question that followed it. As would be expected, the inclusion of this unknown word caused some confusion for Olivia as she struggled to answer this otherwise simple question: "The passage notes all of the following as problems that the **fledgling** Amazon guitar industry has experienced EXCEPT that...." **Fledgling**, as an adjective, means "inexperienced," in that something is considered new or novel. As a noun, **fledgling** can also refer to an inexperienced individual, or a baby bird just about to leave its nest for the first time.

---

**bureaucrats, circumscribed, concede, deterred, electorate
judiciary, layman, legitimacy, perquisites, populace**

---

**bureaucrats** (n.)   members of an administrative policy-making group; nonelected government officials; government characterized by specialization of functions, adherence to fixed rules, and a hierarchy of authority

Red tape and inefficient **bureaucrats** slow down processes that might otherwise be carried out expeditiously and seamlessly.

Both gubernatorial candidates promised to streamline the state's policymaking and to enlist the expertise of efficient, broad-minded **bureaucrats**.

**Bureaucracy** is characterized by a rigid system of administration marked by official sets of procedures and rules.

**circumscribed** (adj.)   limited, restricted in terms of the scope and range of an activity or role; made narrow or tightly defined

The graduate's choices were **circumscribed** because her parents did not want her to attend college out of state.

For Jake, the managerial role was unfulfilling, largely due to its rigid and **circumscribed** job description.

For some, a country lifestyle feels **circumscribed**, causing them to feel penned in and confined.

**concede** (v.)   to grant as a right or privilege; to accept as true, valid, or accurate; to relinquish grudgingly or hesitantly; to yield, give in

More often than not, the right of a business organization to have bylaws is generally **conceded**.

After having his arm twisted by his brother, Jorge finally **conceded** that Carlos had a valid business plan and vision for expansion.

A creature of habit who thrives on continuity, Ms. Irving is not mentally prepared to **concede** her role as Corresponding Secretary of the school board.

**deterred** (v.)   prevented an individual from acting; turned aside; discouraged; dissuaded; impeded; hindered, hampered

Although many dissuaded him from attending medical school because of the lengthy graduate program and residency, his admirable resolve to become a doctor was not **deterred**.

To gain admissions into the joint degree program, a candidate must fulfill a large number of prerequisites; still, the diligent student should not be **deterred**.

Commercials about the illnesses and hardships caused by smoking are meant to **deter** viewers from starting or continuing this unhealthy habit.

**electorate** (n.)   voting population in its entirety; electors; the voting public

An open-minded and well-informed **electorate** is more likely to lead to a judicious election.

To win the approval of the **electorate**, the Congresswoman campaigned tirelessly and never neglected to answer a single question posed to her.

The **electorate** in that particular voting district was easily swayed by the media, whose presentation was both warped and one-sided.

**judiciary** (n.)   a system of courts of law and the judges who preside over them; a branch of government in which judicial power is given

The mediation of disputes and the pursuit of justice are the main roles of any **judiciary**.

A **judiciary** court or assembly follows trial procedures in the company of a judge, litigants, witnesses, jurors, and clerks.

Supreme, local, and municipal courts make up the **judiciary**, or judicial branch of government.

**layman** (n.)   an individual who lacks specialized knowledge of or training in a particular field

To a non-techie **layman**, creating a website from scratch can be a daunting undertaking.

A self-confessed **layman** in home improvement, Hugo lacked specialized training in the fields of plumbing, electricity, and carpentry.

"Professor Sharp, would you kindly delineate the intricacies of the Internet's global structure and workings in **layman's** terms?" pleaded the wide-eyed, befuddled student.

**legitimacy** (n.)   the quality or the state of being legitimate, lawful, and right; pertaining to conditions that are in compliance with the law

The **legitimacy** of the pending lawsuit was questionable.

The attorney will only do pro bono work for cases that she acknowledges as having **legitimacy**.

Most other companies did not recognize the **legitimacy** of the commission.

**perquisite** (n.)   a perk, as in a fringe benefit or an extra; a frill or privilege given to an individual as an exclusive right

A **perquisite** of a job in the fashion industry is being able to attend invitation-only sample sales and trunk shows.

Attending the country club gala is one of the media relations employees' many **perquisites**.

Often people take jobs more for the **perquisites** offered by the company than for the appeal of a 9-to-5 workday.

**populace** (n.)   the masses, general population of individuals; the common people or plebeians

In the cobblestone courtyard, the fiery voices of the **populace** resounded, so that every government official could hear their pleas for justice.

The recession has caused a great sector of the **populace** to suffer greatly, both in terms of economics and planning for the future.

The commoners, also referred to as the general **populace**, sought out every opportunity to have their voices heard by the high-ranking officials.

## MEMORY TIPS

Use these mnemonics (memory devices) to boost your vocabulary. Make up your own memory clues for words in this lesson that are personally challenging. Add these tips, and your own, to your Vocabulary Notebook.

### <u>circum</u>scribed

Let *circum-* remind you of *circum*ference, the length of the line around a circle. Consider the use of this prefix in additional words such as *circum*vent, *circum*navigate, and *circum*locution. Connect this prefix to *scribe*, which means "a writer or copier of text." Knowledge of these stem words will help you piece together and recall this word's meaning more easily.

### <u>leg</u>itimate

Let the *leg-* at the beginning of this word remind you of the word *leg*al, which is a viable synonym in many contexts of this word's use; for example, legitimate business affairs, legitimate claims to property, and legitimate concerns about someone's motives. Legitimate grounds for suing a company, for example, are those that are lawful and right; in other words, they relate to that which is legally sound and in compliance with the law.

### perquisite

Link this lengthy word to its short and sweet definition: *perk*. Simply swap out the *q* for a *k* and you've got this simple definition! Just to review, a *perk* is a bonus, an extra, or a benefit that one receives through employment or some other affiliation. A *perk* is always a plus!

### populace

Let the whole word remind you of <u>popu*la*tion</u>. In Latin, *populous* refers to population. Consider how anything *popular* tends to be well-liked and embraced by the majority of the population.

## MATCHING

Match the vocabulary words in Column A with their defining characteristics in Column B.

**Column A**

1. populace
2. bureaucrats
3. layman
4. concede
5. deterred

**Column B**

A. an extra; a fringe benefit

B. to give up one's role, to give in; to relinquish

C. population of a given area

D. restricted or limited

E. government officials or administrators

F. prevented, blocked from doing something

G. an individual who lacks special training or knowledge

## WORDS IN CONTEXT

Based on the context in which each **bold** word is used, identify the word usage of each sentence as either C (Correct) or I (Incorrect).

1. To understand the intricate workings of Java Script, Pascal, and other sophisticated computer languages, consult with a **layman**.

2. **Deterred** by her nervous friend from taking an ATV tour across the rocky desert, free-spirited Frieda still regrets passing up this thrilling outdoor adventure!

3. Julianna's study-abroad opportunities were rigidly **circumscribed**; she was told that she could spend two semesters overseas in any countries that her heart most desired!

4. The untenable argument lacks **legitimacy**, for it is primarily comprised of hearsay and opinion.

5. After serving five consecutive years as Graduation Chairperson for the eighth grade, Ellen **conceded** her role to an enthusiastic mother who just moved to the school district.

# Lesson 7

## Test Takers' Anecdotes

On a Social Science passage, Julie incorrectly answered a word-in-context question. She had trouble determining how the word, **liability**, was used in context. Even out of context, this word was perplexing for her. A **liability** is a legal responsibility, a burden, or some type of problem that can weigh heavily on a person's shoulders. In this multiple-choice question, the four answer choices were given as follows: *obligation, drawback, probability*, and *result*. Julie mentioned that she also wasn't clear on the meaning of **drawback** (a disadvantage or downside to some circumstance or situation), making this same question further challenging for her.

Sean had some trouble working through the set of reading questions for a Social Science passage. Based on a passage excerpted from an article titled "Green Music in the Rainforest," the questions alone contain the following words: **sustainable, deforestation, inferred, skeptical, dismayed, ventures, intuition, fledgling**, and **ebony**. Sean commented that he would have been able to work through the questions more quickly and much more accurately had he a firmer working knowledge of these words.

---

**alleged, credulity, creed, disavows, harbingers
imminent, quasi, sentiments, spawned, sacrilegious**

---

**alleged** (adj.)   assumed to be true, stated, but not proven to have occurred or be as indicated; supposed, suspected

> The **alleged** criminal sought guidance from his trusted attorneys.

> **Allegedly**, Allen was embezzling funds from the corporation for which he had worked for years.

> The dieticians and nutritionists passionately debated the **alleged** ill effects of both processed and "white" foods.

**credulity** (n.)   gullibility; the tendency to believe in what is said or said to be true; naiveté

> When an individual speaks in one manner while behaving in another, her **credulity** becomes questionable.

> Known for her **credulity**, Gretchen gives credence to almost everything she hears; unfortunately, she also extends a naïve and trusting ear to the town's rumor and gossip.

> Easily duped and deceived, **Credulous** Cleo is not the best partner for his like-minded coworker, Gullible Gus.

**creed** (n.)   a set of beliefs and guiding principles held by an individual or by a group of individuals

> "Live, Love, Laugh" and "To each his own" are two of the positive and harmonious **creeds** by which she lives!

> Vital to the **creed** of the Volunteer Firefighters Organization is the belief that protection of human life is central to being human.

> The Mormons live by a stringent **creed** that renounces many habits and values held by contemporary society.

**disavows** (v.)   to refuse to accept or acknowledge responsibility for having said or done something; to repudiate; to disclaim

> The homeowner's association **disavowed** him, saying that Mr. McKee was not a member and never paid his monthly dues.

> Caught in a web of lies, she now struggles to **disavow** her earlier explanation of events.

> Vehemently, Director Davis **disavowed** the faulty actions of his workers in training.

**harbingers** (n.)   signs of things to come; one who initiates a major change; a precursor; something that or one who presages or foreshadows what is to come

> The new business development was a **harbinger** of affluent times to follow.

> For some, a black crow is a **harbinger** of something negative to come; for others, a black crow is a compelling specimen of nature's strength and beauty.

> Ignoring **harbingers** of financial strain, the couple continued to take lavish vacations and live large.

**imminent** (adj.)   about to or ready to take place, particularly in a threatening manner

> Dishearteningly, hospice patients face gradual and **imminent** death.

> As one home after another was broken into within their neighborhood, the family felt that a break-in at their own house was **imminent**.

> Facing **imminent** danger and hearing howling in the deep dark woods, the campers quickly backtracked toward the campsite.

**quasi** (adj.)   characterized by some resemblance, especially as by possession of specific attributes; almost or nearly

> Though not official and legitimate, the neighbors formed a **quasi**-partnership as they strived to get their avant-garde clothing line off the ground.

> Kyle and Chandra considered theirs a **quasi**-marriage; they cohabitated, shared household chores, but did not possess a marriage license.

> **Quasi**-religious people may not visit their places of worship weekly, yet they may be good people who make the world a better place.

**sacrilegious** (adj.)   disrespectfully treating something regarded as sacred or holy; blasphemous

It is **sacrilegious** to be ungenerous with one's help and time while, at the same time, claiming to be spiritually magnanimous.

**Sacrilegious** acts are revealed in the end, exposing their lack of truth and integrity.

For the ice-cream lover, denaturing those divine scoops with sprinkles, melted marshmallow, and gummy candies amounts to culinary **sacrilege**.

**sentiments** (n.)   ideas and thoughts that are based on feelings and emotions; opinions and points of view that are predominant among a group of people; sentiments can be based on the five senses

More important than the purchased greeting card are the **sentiments** written inside.

False **sentiments** are easily detected by one who is well tuned in to another's genuine personality and values.

What are your **sentiments** regarding studying abroad during your sophomore year of college?

**spawned** (v.)   produced, generated; gave birth to or rise to something

Watching *Shark Tank* can **spawn** new invention and business ideas; after months of brainstorming and fine-tuning their ideas, the viewers' business plans were officially **spawned** and given legal names.

At Long Island's Cold Spring Harbor Fish Hatchery, a new breed of trout was **spawned**.

King prawns tend to **spawn** all year long while tiger prawns primarily **spawn** during the warmer months of spring and summer.

## MEMORY TIPS

Use these mnemonics (memory devices) to boost your vocabulary. Make up your own memory clues for words in this lesson that are personally challenging. Add these tips, and your own, to your Vocabulary Notebook.

### credulity

*Cred-* means "believe." Consider the meaning of this prefix as used in *creed, credo, credit, credence, incredible,* and *incredulous.* Individuals who are known for their **credulity**, tend to believe most of what they hear. To an extent, these people can be considered gullible.

### disavows

The prefix *dis-* indicates "negation, a lacking of, or a reversal." He who **disavows** his statements rescinds or takes back what he has said. In a sense, he is "reversing" his words. Consider the use of *dis-* in these words: *disconnect, disembark, dissimilar, disengage, distrust,* and *disrespect.*

### sacrilegious

The final three syllables of this word sound like *religious.* Use this sound-alike clue to connect you to the meaning of this word: "irreverent, heretical, blasphemous."

### spawn

Did you know that another name for shrimp is *prawn*? Prawns come in several varieties, such as king prawns and tiger prawns. Calling all auditory and visual learners: Allow yourselves to hear and see the word *prawn* within **spawn**. Think of *prawns spawn*ing in the ocean waters. The similar look and sound of these words will help you recall the meaning of **spawn**.

## MATCHING

Match the vocabulary words in Column A with their defining characteristics in Column B.

| Column A | Column B |
|---|---|
| 1. spawned | A. feelings and emotions |
| 2. harbingers | B. a guiding set of principles and beliefs |
| 3. quasi | C. repudiates; disclaims what one has said or promised |
| 4. credulity | |
| 5. creed | D. resembling somebody or something in some ways, but not precisely the same |
| | E. readily and fairly easily believing in something or giving credence to someone's words; gullibility; naiveté |
| | F. developed from the earliest stage |
| | G. precursor, that which foretells |

## WORDS IN CONTEXT

Based on the context in which each **bold** word is used, identify the word usage of each sentence as either C (Correct) or I (Incorrect).

1. The **quasi**-pool club attracted guests seven days a week, as there was neither a membership fee nor a set of rules.

2. "You need to read and heed the **creed** in order to become part of our breed!" bellowed the fraternity pledge leader.

3. **Sacrilegious** religious leaders are likely to attract a congregation of hypocrites.

4. To cleanse himself of negative emotions, Ethan wrote down his heavy **sentiments** in a journal.

5. **Harbingers** of doom, Naysayer Nellie and Worrywart Walter announced a list of the latest imminent calamities about to befall the community.

# Lesson 8

## Test Takers' Anecdotes

A serious and astute student, Elyssa found herself grappling with a Social Science passage question. Her struggle was mainly caused by the fact that she didn't know two of the words that appeared in the answer choices: **contempt** and **feigned**. She ended up erroneously choosing "silent **contempt**" as her answer. Elyssa mistakenly associated the word *contempt* with happiness, because she phonetically connected it to the word *content*. Had she known the true meaning of **contempt** (scorn, hatred, disrespect), she would not have selected this answer and she would have had a stronger shot at getting this question right.

When reading a Social Science passage taken from Eleanor Roosevelt's biography, Wilson expressed some hesitation when he ran into a plethora (abundance) of potentially challenging vocabulary words. Words included **integrity**, **distinct**, **forefront**, **mentors**, **pacifist**, **forestall**, and **agitators**. He diligently made flash cards and then continued on with the passage. Wilson continued to express his unease when he came across phrases such as "**championed** a New Deal," "**engineered** policy," "ER **lobbied**," "she **courted radicals**," "her **abiding conviction**," and "**progressive pioneers**." This passage was an eye-opener for Wilson, who now clearly understands the importance of building his vocabulary in order to achieve his personal best score on the ACT.

---

bequeaths, durable, ecologist, emissions, harvested
mutual, onus, prototype, revel, streamlined

---

**bequeaths** (v.)   to leave property to someone after death by means of a will; to hand down something such as knowledge to future generations

> To her twin nieces, Anne **bequeathed** flower-shaped gold and pearl pendants.

> To each of her loved ones, she **bequeathed** traditional furnishings, collectibles, and antiques.

> Priceless pearls of wisdom were **bequeathed** to her son, daughters, and nine grandchildren.

**durable** (adj.)   long lasting; enduring; lasting for a long while without experiencing wear and tear or damage

> Their home was made of **durable** materials: brick, granite, porcelain tile, and hardwoods.

> Fond of spiral notebooks with **durable** covers, Phillip prefers not to use the ones whose covers are made of cardboard.

> In long term estate planning, **durable** power of attorney requires the individual to choose his or her health care agent if the individual becomes incapacitated or incapable of making sound decisions.

**ecologist** (n.)   one who studies or specializes in a branch of science concerned with the interrelationship of organisms and their environments; one who studies intricate systems such as that of language or patterns between organisms and their habitats

> The **ecologist** documented the relationships between food webs and their natural environments.

> The geneticist, the human **ecologist**, and the behavioral scientist will meet at a national consortium whose mission is to improve the quality of life of those living in poverty.

To the astute **ecologist**, all aspects of a system are worthy of analysis, including the health of the environment, population patterns, and recycling efforts that may or may not be in place.

**emissions** (n.)   something given out or released, such as harmful exhausts; discharges

To protect one's thyroid from potentially damaging radiation **emissions** during a dental examination, the patient should wear a chest and throat guard.

If the exposed insulation is manipulated, its **emissions** can irritate and ultimately be harmful to one's lungs.

Potentially deadly, carbon monoxide **emissions** often go undetected by homeowners.

**harvested** (v.)   gathered a crop for the purpose of sale or use; killed animals for the purpose of food, as sport, to sell, or to control their population

Herbs and plants such as aloe, lavender, and lemon verbena may be **harvested** for medicinal and therapeutic purposes.

Was that pecan-crusted bass on your dinner plate **harvested** from a storm water pond or caught in a wild fishery?

**Harvested** for their meat, which is used for human consumption, snapping turtles are detrimentally affected by large commercial **harvests**.

**mutual** (adj.)   shared or felt by two people; expressed or done with regard to the other; reciprocal

**Mutual** respect and responsibility are indispensable features in any sound and genuine partnership, whether business or personal.

"I love you, and you love me." The feeling is **mutual**.

A self-centered life and one devoted to others are **mutually** exclusive ways of living.

**onus** (n.) a burden or responsibility; one's duty or obligation

The **onus** is on each individual to find happiness and balance in his or her life.

Together, they tackled the **onerous** task of cleaning out the overstuffed backyard shed.

In a healthy partnership or marriage, both parties should mutually share responsibilities; in other words, they should bear the **onus** as a team.

**prototype** (n.) the original form of something that has essentially the same features and characteristics of later forms of that same type; the epitome

The original test day kit **prototype** contained a Vitamin E lip balm, a vitamin C lollipop, and a roll of Mentos mints.

Before acquiring a patent, each inventor must create a tangible **prototype** of the product or innovation.

Using stretchable, patterned fabrics, Dana created several **prototypes** of her stylish book covers.

**revel** (v.) to experience something with great pleasure; to enjoy a gathering or party in a festive way; to celebrate in a lively, even loud, manner

The lively and festive group of neighborhood friends danced, ate, and chatted indefatigably as they **reveled** in the fun at the Summer Sizzler party!

Some guests swam, cheered, and **reveled** garrulously in the free-form pool!

The **revels** at the beach club began at seven thirty and ended at two in the morning with a salvo of fireworks.

**streamlined** (v.) made more efficient by making a business, process, or organization more simplified, modernized, or updated

Once the executive directors had put a simple set of steps in place, the daily workings of their business became time-efficient and **streamlined**.

Wearing primarily black and white and very few accessories, Angela **streamlined** her wardrobe.

A **streamlined** production process yields higher net profits.

---

## MEMORY TIPS

Use these mnemonics (memory devices) to boost your vocabulary. Make up your own memory clues for words in this lesson that are personally challenging. Add these tips, and your own, to your Vocabulary Notebook.

### durable
Consider how the word root *dura* suggests the idea of "long lasting" in words you may know such as en*dura*nce, *dura*tion, and en*dura*e. Have you heard of Duraflame® fire logs or Duracell batteries? The *dura-* prefix accentuates the long-lasting flames, which are perfect for a campfire or roasting pit. Likewise, *dura-* calls attention to the long-lasting power of the batteries.

### onus
Imagine two buddies talking:

"Hey, Buddy, the **onus** is *on us* to get this job done."

"Yep, I know. I feel the **onus** on our shoulders."

"Think positive! If we take seriously this **onus**, we are more likely to receive that b*onus*!"

### streamlined
Picture a stream running through a forest. If you're like most, you probably picture a meandering pathway of water with lots of ins and outs, bends and curves. Now imagine that same stream straightened out into a simple *line*. The stream has been **streamlined** or simplified in your mind's eye! Use this visual clue to cement the meaning of this word in your memory.

## MATCHING

Match the vocabulary words in Column A with their defining characteristics in Column B.

| Column A | Column B |
|---|---|
| 1. revel | A. made a process simpler, more straightforward |
| 2. harvested | B. the original model or form |
| 3. streamlined | C. to delight in something or someone |
| 4. bequeaths | D. killed animals to control their population |
| 5. durable | E. lasting a long time and showing minimal wear |
|  | F. bestows a gift |
|  | G. one who studies systems and webs of life |

## WORDS IN CONTEXT

Based on the context in which each **bold** word is used, identify the word usage of each sentence as either C (Correct) or I (Incorrect).

1. Thomas and his dad **harvested** a half dozen deer from the upstate woods to help retard the spread of Lyme disease.

2. The **ecologist** studies fascinating topics such as time travel, black holes, and galaxy expansion.

3. The committee **streamlined** their hiring process from three steps to six.

4. **Mutual** respect is an indispensable key to any long-lasting and positive relationship.

5. The teenagers **reveled** in the attractions and delectable treats at St. Rocco's Feast, including the Cyclone Ride, Dragon Coaster, funnel cakes, and fried double-stuffed Oreos!

# Lesson 9

## Test Takers' Anecdotes

Many students answer this Social Science question incorrectly: "The author calls which of the following an **anomaly**?" Because these students have no clue what **anomaly** means, they end up feeling out of their depths and they just guess on this question. **Anomaly** means "rarity or irregularity, as it applies to a particular circumstance," and it's a handy word to know at test time!

In another Social Science passage about psychology as it pertains to human growth and development, students found a bevy of challenging words. They included: **maturation, attributes, optic, devised, peering, profusion, neurons, attain, vague,** and **speculation**. Phrases woven throughout the passage contained a challenging word or two: "mice **reared** in the dark," "**differentiate** among **hues**," "an **offsetting** advantage," "make...fine **distinctions**," and "**impaired sensory** performance." On top of all this, a few sophisticated science words were defined in the passage, including **stereopsis, dendrites,** and **synapses**.

---

> **allocate, barren, bias, constitute, infrastructure**
> **inordinate, mandate, objective, obliterating, utility**

---

**allocate** (v.)   apportion, distribute evenly; to set something aside for a specific purpose or person; assign; allot

> The scholarship committee sought to **allocate** its funds evenly among the caddie scholarship recipients.

> There are limited hours in any given day; mindfully **allocate** your time to productive and positive pursuits.

> Allison **allocates** an hour per day to working out, a couple hours to errands, and during the remaining hours she lives up to her motto, "Born to Shop!"

**barren** (adj.)   not producing or incapable of producing; infertile; empty; fruitless; unproductive

> "Does anyone live here?" she wondered to herself. "This house feels **barren**."

> The expanse of beefsteak tomato plants, lush basil, and eggplants was a mirage. In actuality, the garden plot was **barren** except for a few stray dandelions.

> The young newlywed was distraught when the gynecologist informed her that she was **barren** and could not have her own biological children.

**bias** (n.)   an opinion or one-sided outlook; a preconceived notion

> Both the Writing multiple-choice questions on the SAT and the English multiple-choice questions on the ACT exhibit a clear **bias** toward language economy.

> Lucky for him, his lifestyle **bias** is slanted toward activity rather than the sedentary existence of a couch potato.

> To avoid **bias** among the voters, they should represent a cross-section of community members.

**constitute** (v.)   to make up the whole or a specific part of something; to be something or to have the status and factors to amount to a particular thing; to be an ingredient of something larger

> What factors, for you personally, **constitute** a desirable quality of life?

> Six individuals of distinction **constituted** the interviewing committee.

> According to Jim, the contract does not **constitute** a fair or reasonable offer of terms and conditions.

**infrastructure** (n.)   an organization's fundamental framework or underlying foundation; the public works of a country, region, or state, including the personnel, structures, buildings, and equipment required to carry out its activities

> To maintain the town's aesthetic appeal, an infusion of cash is needed to rehabilitate its decrepit-looking **infrastructure**.

> The city's deteriorating **infrastructure** is in dire need of a facelift.

> Along with *asphalt, blueprints, cantilever,* and *scaffolding,* **infrastructure** is a term relevant to the field of civil engineering.

**inordinate** (adj.)   beyond a reasonable degree, measure, or limit; excessive

> Although she shopped for an **inordinate** supply of food, snacks, clothing, and toiletries each week, there always seemed to be more to buy for her household.

> Farrah, a fashionista, spends an **inordinate** amount of money on sweaters, purses, boots, and other fashion accessories.

> An **inordinate** amount of money is required to attend undergraduate and graduate school.

**mandate** (n.)   a command or formal order that is stated with authority; authorization to act that is given to a representative of the people

> Speaking as if she were a royal, she made it clear to her subordinates that her **mandates** must be obeyed or the consequences will be grave.

> The construction company fulfilled the mayor's **mandate** to build more lanes for merging on and off the busy highway.

**objective** (adj.)   observable; based on facts or conditions that are perceived without personal feelings, prejudices, or interpretations; without individual opinion; derived from the senses or experiences with actual objects and circumstances

> The scientists could use someone outside the institute to provide them with an **objective** analysis of their organization.

> "Leave your opinions and reveries at the door," Dr. Goji announced. "Today's lab analysis will be solely an **objective** assessment based on the concrete results of our experimentation."

> Answer the question **objectively**; please leave your emotions and desires out of your response.

> Pre-med majors study a wealth of **objective** material based on experiment-based facts, observation, and empirical evidence.

**obliterating** (v.)   eradicating; removing completely from memory, existence, or recognition; to destroy all indication of; to cause to collapse or disappear

> The hailstorm **obliterated** their plans to assemble a set of hammocks under the towering oak tree in their backyard.

> Slowly, they **obliterated** every trace of interaction with that side of the family, as if the Hannons never existed.

> In an effort to **obliterate** plagiarism, some high school teachers require students to submit their term papers to turnitin.com before reading and evaluating them.

**utility** (n.)   usefulness; fitness for attaining some purpose, worth, or outcome; something useful; a service (light, power, or water) provided by a public utility

> The basement **utility** room was filled to the gills with assorted items useful for homeowners: a wet vacuum, a dehumidifier, and a large tool organizer.

> Gus took his **utility** knife with him whenever he went camping or fishing. He could use it to cut fishing line, to open a can of food, or to clean his catch of the day!

> His plan is convoluted and undefined; it lacks **utility**.

## MEMORY TIPS

Use these mnemonics (memory devices) to boost your vocabulary. Make up your own memory clues for words in this lesson that are personally challenging. Add these tips, and your own, to your Vocabulary Notebook.

### barren

Think *bare* (empty, vacant, blank, lacking) when you read and hear *barren*. A field "bare" of corn and wheat is a barren field. A woman who is **barren** cannot have children. An author who cannot think of topics to write about finds himself **barren** of ideas and inspiration.

### inordinate

The prefix *in-* means "not." So, simply break down *inordinate* to mean "not ordinary." For example, an **inordinate** number of required volunteer hours or an **inordinate** price for a pair of boots is beyond reason, immoderate, or excessive. Knowledge of this prefix and stem word will help you piece together and recall this word's meaning.

## MATCHING

Match the vocabulary words in Column A with their defining characteristics in Column B.

| Column A | Column B |
|---|---|
| 1. barren | A. to erase, remove, eradicate |
| 2. bias | B. a law or order; a decree |
| 3. obliterate | C. an opinion or preference |
| 4. mandate | D. infertile; lacking growth or a harvest |
| 5. allocate | E. to apportion; to give to each a share; to ration or evenly distribute |
| | F. excessive; out of the normal range or expectation |

## WORDS IN CONTEXT

Based on the context in which each **bold** word is used, identify the word usage of each sentence as either C (Correct) or I (Incorrect).

1. Unlike subjective statements, **objective** comments are those that more often tend to lead to arguments.

2. The declutterer's mantra states, "Keep an item only if it is something of value, beauty, or **utility**."

3. Bridges, tunnels, and highways comprise a city's **infrastructure**.

4. Although he says that personality counts, Shallow Sid's **bias** is toward people's outward appearance.

5. Once brimming with tomato plants, string beans, and cucumber vines, the garden plot is cold and **barren** in late November.

# Lesson 10

## Test Takers' Anecdotes

Harry encountered some difficulty in the opening paragraphs of a Social Science passage about making stringed instruments out of wood. In the first few paragraphs alone, his reading was slowed down a bit by his lack of facility with words such as: **acronym**, **burgeoning**, **rural**, **urbanizing**, **stewardship**, and **council**. Vocabulary strength would have increased not only his speed but also his accuracy in answering reading comprehension questions.

As Jill read aloud from a Social Science passage about climate change and how these changes affected history, she expressed how she found the reading interesting. The passage held her interest. However, as she read, she stumbled somewhat upon encountering these words whose meanings were cloudy to her: **mammoth**, **devoid**, **prolonged**, **anomaly**, **proxy**, **bewildering**, **intricate**, **fiefdom**, **archaeologists**, **determinism**, **notion**, **academia**, **causative**, **subsistence**, **dearth**, and **ineptitude**.

---

**courtiers, depict, erroneous, façade, flaw**

**intact, notable, ravages, simulation, tableau**

---

**courtiers** (n.)    officials of a royal court; aristocrats who attend a queen or king; individuals who spend time in the royal court; individuals who flatter others; sycophants

> The monarch was visibly irritated that his meal looked and tasted identical to that enjoyed by his **courtiers**.

> Prior to becoming a **courtier** to King Louis XIV, Nathaniel owned a violin strings manufacturing company.

> The queen's **courtiers** catered to her every whim, serving her tea and cucumber sandwiches while they fanned her and read her letters aloud.

**depict** (v.)   to describe or portray through words or an artistic form such as a painting or picture; to illustrate or represent

> An alluring travel writer, Juanita chooses her words artfully when she **depicts** the exotic places across the globe she has visited.

> Situated right on the water, The Harbor Bath Club is so scenic and peaceful that it is hard to **depict** its natural beauty in words; only panoramic pictures can do it justice.

> Aesthetically and in terms of layout and flow, how might you **depict** your dream home?

**erroneous** (adj.)   faulty, misleading; containing error, inaccuracies, or misinformation; faultily interpreted or presented

> **Erroneous** data obscured the research findings about a rare form of thyroid cancer.

> Despite the inclusion of **erroneous** details, the forensic detective's account seemed credible.

> A two-hour delay in their road trip to the Jersey Shore was caused by Fredrick's **erroneous** driving directions.

**façade** (n.)   a false exterior; the front of a building; a deceptive appearance or manner; a pretense or outward show, as in someone's public image

> For Fiona the Fake, keeping up a picture-perfect **façade** occupies her every waking moment.

> Hannah's calm and easy **façade** belies her inner unrest.

> The brick **façade** of the donation center withstood substantial damage during the hurricane.

**flaw** (n.)   an imperfection or defect in appearance, character, or based on some system or whole; a detracting feature, trait, or characteristic

Hubris, an overwhelming sense of pride, was the protagonist's main character **flaw**.

Haughty Haily's self-centered disposition is an unfortunate personality **flaw**.

Law Professor Kelly scrutinized his student's fifteen-page brief, trying to detect **flaws** in the written document.

**intact** (adj.)   undamaged, without missing or broken parts; whole, complete; untouched in its original form or state

Although the teenager had a dozen friends over, the basement recreation room remained miraculously **intact**.

Despite the torrential rain and intense wind gusts of Hurricane Sandy, the Carne's home and yard was astonishingly left **intact**.

Mother's cherub collection is sentimental and precious. Unwilling to part with any one, each family member gave a cherub sculpture a home, keeping the collection **intact**.

**notable** (adj.)   remarkable; meriting attention because of its interest, importance, or significance; noteworthy

Excerpts from the student's **notable** research will be published in Dr. Geller's next book.

Most **notable** of his oil paintings is the abstract of dancers who appear as if they are in motion and feeling the music.

Miranda's most **notable** asset is her personality: she consistently exudes a resilient and positive attitude.

**ravages** (n.)   acts of destruction or plundering; the damaging effects of something

*The Impossible* is a movie that vividly and heart-wrenchingly depicts the **ravages** of the Tsunami that struck southeast Asia in 2009.

Despite the **ravages** of the hurricane, the family felt gratitude for being together, safe and sound.

The **ravages** of weather, time, and the settling of the foundation eroded the steps made of slate, mortar, and brick.

**simulation** (n.)   the imitation or reproduction of something's characteristic features; an artificial object or process; something that feels real but is not; replication, recreation

Some of Walt Disney World's most exciting attractions are the ones that heavily use **simulation**, along with sound and visual effects.

The submarine **simulation** ride was one of her favorites. She felt as if she were a deep sea explorer!

Awing the inquisitive kindergartners, a simple experiment using carbonated beverages and Mentos mints **simulates** a chemical reaction resembling an explosion.

**tableau** (n.)   a vivid, picturesque description or display; a dramatic situation or scene that arises; a montage; an artistic or striking arrangement, grouping, or scene

Shobha's collage of candid photos made a compelling **tableau** on Instagram.

The pre-prom red carpet was held at the Sands Point Preserve mansion, providing a stunning **tableau** for the high school couples.

The evening gambol premiered with its traditional Red Carpet event, an exciting **tableau** during which each prom couple steps out of their limo, poses for photos, then walks the red carpet to the castle entrance!

## MEMORY TIPS

Use these mnemonics (memory devices) to boost your vocabulary. Make up your own memory clues for words in this lesson that are personally challenging. Add these tips, and your own, to your Vocabulary Notebook.

### courtiers

Let *court*, which is built in to this word, remind you of attendants to the royal *court,* where **courtiers** are apt (likely) to be found.

### erroneous

Let the first four letters lead you to picture a word you undoubtedly know: *error.* **Erroneous** research findings are faulty because they contain *error.* Likewise, **erroneous** conclusions can be misleading, murky, or downright false.

### façade

To review, a **façade** is a deceptive or false appearance. Think of the human *face* as a type of mask or *façade*, a false cover or exterior. Some individuals conceal their emotions of sadness or desperation behind a cheerful smile. Likewise, some conceal their insecurities behind other facial expressions, such as a grimace, scowl, frown, or snarl. For example, imagine someone's congenial conversation and pleasant face as merely a **façade** for the deception that lurks within.

### ravages

Link this word to a rhyming word that you already know, *savages*. Now picture a vivid scene in which *savages* are the cause of sweeping **ravages** (destruction, ruin, fires…) experienced by the ransacked village!

### simulation

Let *sim* lead you to the word *similar*. A **simulation** creates a situation or effect that feels *similar* to the actual thing. At the Atlantis Marine World aquarium in Riverhead, Long Island, New York, there is a *simulated* submarine ride that is a big attraction for guests. Likewise, St. Luke's feast offers a towering and spine-tingling ride *simulating* bungee jumping!

## MATCHING

Match the vocabulary words in Column A with their defining characteristics in Column B.

| Column A | Column B |
|---|---|
| 1. erroneous | A. faulty, misleading, containing error |
| 2. intact | B. strife, discord, lack of harmony |
| 3. ravages | C. a dramatic, visually alluring scene |
| 4. dissonance | D. remarkable based on value, merit, or talent |
| 5. tableau | E. in its original form, undamaged |
| | F. to portray or describe in words |
| | G. damages, destruction |

## WORDS IN CONTEXT

Based on the context in which each **bold** word is used, identify the word usage of each sentence as either C (Correct) or I (Incorrect).

1. Hanna's **ravages** need to be fed twice a day and have their cages cleaned weekly.

2. The **tableau** was elegantly set with fine bone china plates, sterling silver cutlery, and embroidered linen napkins.

3. Xbox One provides sports animations and **simulations** that make players feel like they're amid the heated action of game day!

4. Following gale force hurricane winds and a pelting downpour of rain, the basketball hoop, trampoline, and soccer nets miraculously remained **intact**!

5. A **notable** bard, he draws a crowd when he recites his free verse poetry at local libraries and coffee shops.

# Part III
# Reading Test:
# Humanities Vocabulary

Topics addressed in this category of passages include excerpts from memoirs and essays. These works may focus on architecture, art, dance, ethics, film, language, literary criticism, music, philosophy, radio, and/or theater.

## Word Bank

The words below are from the Humanities section of ACT practice exams. These words have all presented some level of difficulty, confusion, or uncertainty for students. This comprehensive list includes words from the passages themselves, from the questions, and from the answer choices. Not every word in this vocabulary bank is included in the following lessons, which feature only ten words each. Only those words that tend to appear most frequently on exams or those that students found the most unclear are examined in depth.

## Humanities Reading Passages

Words listed appear within the passages and/or their corresponding questions. **Test 1**: abounds, affiliations, anthology, compatriots, consciousness, disavow, discriminatory, enumerate, expatriate, glibness, inexhaustible, inherently, insinuated, mainstream, melancholy, nostalgia, obscure, obscures, overtly, phantom, repressive, rudimentary, sovereign, superficial; **Test 2**: alienation, awestruck, conformity, detached, deterrence, eloquently, endured, fandom, foresight, inauguration, inferred, intact, languished, memoirs, meteoric, nonetheless, paradox, percolate, phenomenon, provocative, optimistic, resonated, rifts, rural, skepticism, spawned, syndicated, unparalleled, unprecedented, urban, visionary; **Test 3**: bemoans, censors, conjure, contemporary, dawning, definitive, demurral, disconcerting, distinct, eerie, enchanting, feverish, inevitably, innovations, intimidated, lush, mediocre, muddled, mutability, profound, reconceived, renditions, restrained, skeptical, static, supplemented, synchronized, verify; **Test 4**: aggregate, annotations, aster, attribute, bog, condescension, cryptic, daunting, ignoramus, indispensable, intricate, kin, quivering, lax, rambles, retrospect; **Test 5**: affirmations, collaborations, connoted, cosmopolitan, demographics, documentary, eclecticism, fond, fusions, hybrids, improvisations, improvisers, indifference, labyrinthine, madcap, merge, mobilizing, mutiny, preceded, premiere, profound, punctuate, recapitulate, rendezvous, resounding, scorn, sprawling, urban.

# Lesson 11

## Test Takers' Anecdotes

In a Humanities reading passage, John missed a multiple-choice question because he erroneously chose this answer: **nostalgia**. Had he understood the meaning of **nostalgia** (a longing for the past, a bittersweet sense of homesickness), he would have realized that it did not fit Armstrong's musical purpose. John commented that the words in the passage made it hard for him to follow; the introductory and concluding paragraphs alone contain: **immaculate**, **virtuosic**, **underpinnings**, **suffused**, **profound**, **antidote**.

In a Humanities passage about French scientist and philosopher Descartes, test taker Shay confronted a few uncomfortable words in just one of the reading questions. Luckily for her, the rest of the questions were not as vocabulary laden. Although she gave the question her best educated guess, having these words in the mix made her feel less confident about her answer choice: **rudimentary**, **obsolete**, and **feats**. If Shay had had facility with these words, the question would have been more accessible for her.

---

> **affiliations, anthology, inexhaustible, inherently, insinuated**
> **mainstream, nostalgia, overtly, phantom, sovereign**

---

**affiliations** (n.)   relationships, alliances; connections with organizations such as those that are religious or political in nature; associations

> Too much involvement and too many **affiliations** can render one's participation flimsy and inconsequential.

> His collegiate **affiliations** at the university include intramural club sports, membership in a fraternity, and a work-study position as a residential director.

> Though each of us is our own person, an individual is still often defined by his or her **affiliations**.

**anthology** (n.)   a collection of short stories and/or poems; sometimes a collection of works of art or musical compositions

> The young man's photograph, "Lone Seagull," was published in a hardcover **anthology** of poems and pictures relating to Long Island.

> Dr. Painter's short literary works and essays make up her award-winning Italian prose collection in an **anthology** titled *A Woman's Voice*.

> Titled *Today's Vibe*, the **anthology** is geared toward a teen audience and contains short stories about shopping at American Apparel, attending concerts, posting on Facebook, and Tweeting.

**inexhaustible** (adj.)   unable to be depleted, used up, or exhausted; tireless; limitless; infinite; boundless

> The Seaside Heights boardwalk offers **inexhaustible** amusements: arcades, souvenir shops, Henna tattoos, and soft-serve ice cream.

> The **inexhaustible** energy of the five-year-old boys was evident during their four-hour play date, during which they played basketball, splashed in the pool, and built race cars attached with magnets.

> Unless her efforts to make amends and to move forward peaceably have been **inexhaustible**, she should try and try again.

**inherently** (adv.)   based on the nature of something or of an individual; essentially part of something's basic nature or character; intrinsically; innately

> The newborn **inherently** knew to hold his breath when submerged under water.

> **Inherently**, Nina had maternal instincts that could not be learned from reading books or attending child-rearing workshops.

> As designed and constructed, what are the **inherent** weaknesses of this building?

**insinuated** (v.)   hinted at something that is unflattering or unpleasant; suggested in an indirect manner; intimated; to wheedle or worm your way into something, such as a membership or organization to which you were not invited

> Maliciously, Aunt Gertrude **insinuated** that her niece was jealous of her cousin!

> Antagonistic toward her neighbor and former friend, Hilde **insinuated** that she couldn't swing a golf club without the undivided assistance of a personal pro.

**mainstream** (adj.)   considered usual, normal, or ordinary by the majority of people; accepted by most people; typical; conventional

> Bucking **mainstream** beach attire, free-spirited Willy wore a tux and red satin cummerbund to the shore!

> Top 40 hits, rather than indie releases, are more likely to be played on **mainstream** radio stations.

> Those parties are over-the-top and considered extraordinary by everyone—they are anything but **mainstream**.

**nostalgia** (n.)   a bittersweet longing for the past; yearning for a time that is irrecoverable; homesickness

> Nothing quite fills a person with **nostalgia** like watching videos from happy days of decades past.

> We are meant to live in the present. Spending too many hours sunk deep in the reverie of **nostalgia** is counterproductive to our well-being.

> On his sixteenth birthday, the sophomore flipped through his grammar school scrapbooks and photo albums, smiling and laughing **nostalgically**.

**overtly** (adv.)   openly; visibly; pertaining to feelings and opinions expressed in a very open and demonstrative way

> **Overtly** enthusiastic about his summer position as camp counselor, Trevor excitedly recounts the activities of his day.

> Wide-eyed and smiling, the young campers exhibit **overt** excitement about Slip-and-Slide, Carnival Day, and beach combing for shells, crab legs, and driftwood.

> Not surprisingly, Oliver's **overtly** warm personality makes him more inclined to exhibit public displays of affection.

**phantom** (n.)   a ghost, apparition, scepter; anything that is not physically present but whose presence can be felt or detected; imagined

> Choosing to ignore the hard realities of her life, she lives a **phantom** existence.

> Justina's **phantom** friends allow her to feel less isolated from her peers.

> In January, the enamored coupled spent an evening dining at Le Cirque and then seeing *Phantom of the Opera* on Broadway.

**sovereign** (adj.)   self-governing; independent; possessing supreme power, authority, or influence

> To protect its autonomy, the **sovereign** nation tends to insulate itself from the influences of its contiguous states.

> Some politicians argue that global welfare is more important than any individual nation's **sovereignty**.

> Cassandra dreamed of becoming the **sovereign** ruler of some great kingdom.

## MEMORY TIPS

Use these mnemonics (memory devices) to boost your vocabulary. Make up your own memory clues for words in this lesson that are personally challenging. Add these tips, and your own, to your Vocabulary Notebook.

### inherently
Link this word to a word you likely already know from biology class: *inherited*. Think of the term, "inherited traits." Note these viable synonyms that all happen to start with *in-*: intrinsically, innately, and instinctively.

### overtly
Slant rhyme **overtly** with *openly*. People who **overtly** express their emotions do so openly and demonstratively. Another tip for remembering this word is to notice that *overt* and *covert* are antonyms. *Covert* means "hidden." (Think "covered.")

## MATCHING

Match the vocabulary words in Column A with their defining characteristics in Column B.

**Column A**

1. mainstream
2. phantom
3. sovereign
4. nostalgia
5. inexhaustible

**Column B**

A. having supreme authority or power

B. common, typical; characteristic of the masses or majority

C. a bittersweet longing for the past

D. ghost-like, an apparition

E. seemingly endless or infinite

F. based on natural ability; innate

## WORDS IN CONTEXT

Based on the context in which each **bold** word is used, identify the word usage of each sentence as either C (Correct) or I (Incorrect).

1. Trying hard to quietly blend into the bustling crowd, Henrietta **overtly** expressed her disapproval of the evening's events.

2. **Nostalgically**, Mr. and Mr. McKee planned out the details of their dream retirement.

3. Valuing money above almost everything else, Dennis worked **inexhaustibly** to build a hefty savings account.

4. To many of us, Mickey Mouse, apple pie, and baseball are part of the fabric of **mainstream** American culture.

5. The **sovereign** government relied on other nations in order to make decisions and put laws into effect.

# Lesson 12

## Test Takers' Anecdotes

The answer choices presented the most difficulty for Georgina. Although she made out fine with the reading of the essay excerpt itself, which was about the Star Trek phenomenon, she felt some uncertainty when she encountered certain phrases among the vocabulary-heavy answer choices. Here are some examples of phrases that tripped her up: "**detached** interest," "mild **skepticism**," "dealt with imagination and **foresight**," and "being **provocative**."

---

**alienation, conformity, escapist, memoirs, paradox
phenomenon, rifts, scope, unparalleled, visionary**

---

**alienation** (n.)   an effect of becoming unfriendly, even hostile; an effect of feeling disconnected or unsupported; estrangement; isolation

> Some people are despondent victims of **alienation**; others seek it as a means of indulging into their quiet and private time.

> **Alienation** from family and friends can cause an individual to become overly self-oriented or lonely.

> Her cold, authoritative disposition gradually **alienated** her from her family.

**conformity** (n.)   compliance with requirements and standards; behavior similar to that of most everybody else; agreement in conduct, structure, or character; sameness, obedience, submission

> A master of **conformity**, Massimo can blend into any crowd.

> "Social **conformity** makes for a dull village," muttered the philosopher.

> Noticeably disconcerted, the boarding school dean detected a lack of **conformity** in young Nate's attitude.

**escapist** (adj.)   furnishing a means of forgetting about and temporarily parting from the difficult or worrisome aspects of reality; tending to avoid reality; dwelling in fantasy

> Running away from their troubled world, Delia and Celia spend long **escapist** days at the beach.

> **Escapist**, nonsensical television that does not require thought or concentration is her favorite.

> The **escapist** does not operate by this creed: "When the going gets tough, the tough get going."

**memoirs** (n.)   a person's written story about his or her life or life events; autobiographical accounts, usually written in a literary fashion

> His casual, hand-written travel journals gradually developed into three artistic volumes of **memoirs**.

> *Brighton Beach **Memoirs*** is a semi-autobiographical play by Neil Simon set in Brooklyn in 1937.

> English teacher Ms. Davis starts her **memoir** writing unit with the story of how she adopted her first puppy, Beckita, from the North Shore Animal League.

**paradox** (n.)   something unexpected, contradictory, ironic, or absurd; an individual with contradictory qualities within him or herself; a statement that contradicts itself; an irony, an illogical statement or situation

"Jumbo shrimp" and "bittersweet" are **paradoxical** terms.

A hard guy to figure out, Christian is a **paradox**. Is he an easygoing Ed or a nervous Ned?

Although nicknamed the Alien Theory, **paradoxically**, there is nothing strange or new about it.

**phenomenon** (n.)   something extraordinary that incites wonder, excitement, and/or awe in people who observe or encounter it; someone who is considered to be exceptional; a marvel; a great wonder or spectacle

The rectangular rainbow that miraculously formed above their home alone is a **phenomenon** that the family will never comprehend.

In Lina's estimation, the meat-eating Venus flytrap plant is one of nature's most wondrous **phenomena**.

Black holes are a **phenomenon** that can engage us in thought and wonder for endless hours.

**rifts** (n.)   gaps or breaks in something where it has split apart; a disagreement or conflict that hampers relationships; displacement of layers of rock in the Earth's crust, resulting from stress and pressure; shallow and flowing water

Sadly, a **rift** in the family gradually developed into deep trenches of hurt that could not be healed.

Geological **rifts** created fault lines on each side of the rugged rock formations.

To avoid **rifts** among team members, Sheila would habitually keep many of her thoughts and feelings to herself.

**scope** (n.)   a range or expanse covered by a subject, topic, or activity; the freedom and space to act; an individual's mental capacity; a breadth, extent, or reach

> Clearly delineate for the admissions office the **scope** of your volunteer work.

> The esoteric question posed to the professor is beyond the **scope** of his studies.

> What is the **scope** of your clinical research?

**unparalleled** (adj.)   unmatched in quality or type; beyond compare; the best of a particular kind; incomparable

> Preparing to become a foreign currency trader, studious Trevor possesses a business acumen that is **unparalleled** among his peers.

> Diva Dee's fashion designs are **unparalleled** in their style, color, and flair.

> The kitchen design is **unparalleled** in its high-end appliances, granite flooring, and custom moldings.

**visionary** (adj.)   having acute foresight and imagination; unrealistic because something is too idealistic or dreamy in nature; (n.) someone who has mystical visions and insights

> The man's **visionary** leadership inspires his family and encourages them that there are many good things to come.

> Vivian is a **visionary** artist who creates unique and stirring works of three-dimensional art, using recyclables from her community.

> The Long Island medium, Theresa Caputo, is a vivacious **visionary** with a great and loyal following.

## MEMORY TIPS

Use these mnemonics (memory devices) to boost your vocabulary. Make up your own memory clues for words in this lesson that are personally challenging. Add these tips, and your own, to your Vocabulary Notebook.

### <u>alien</u>ation
Imagine how an alien would feel if he found himself sitting among you and your classmates in AP Bio or among you and your friends in Period 7 lunch! He would feel out of place or out of his comfort zone. (Is he more comfortable on Mars?) Now, link this visual story to the definition of **alienation**, which is "an uncomfortable feeling of distance or estrangement."

### memoirs
Let the sound and look of the word **memoirs** remind you of *memories*. To a great extent, memoir writers rely on their *memories* for their creative, narrative material.

### <u>vision</u>ary
Focus on *vision* when you encounter the word **visionary**. Possessing some degree of extrasensory perception, a **visionary**, to an arguable extent, can *envision* or see aspects of the future.

## MATCHING

Match the vocabulary words in Column A with their defining characteristics in Column B.

| Column A | Column B |
|---|---|
| 1. conformity | A. sameness; striving to be of the same type or kind |
| 2. rifts | |
| 3. phenomenon | B. a crafted story of one's personal past that typically contains anecdotes |
| 4. visionary | C. divides; conflicts that break apart what was once together |
| 5. memoirs | D. isolation; feeling alone and set apart from others |
| | E. a seer, soothsayer, or clairvoyant |
| | F. pertaining to a departure from reality |
| | G. a great wonder or unexplained occurrence |

## WORDS IN CONTEXT

Based on the context in which each **bold** word is used, identify the word usage of each sentence as either C (Correct) or I (Incorrect).

1. Samantha indulged in **escapist** reading by perusing the cover stories in *The New York Times* business section.

2. Mia's **memoir** was about the life of Copernicus and his scientific findings.

3. Connor the **Conformist** prided himself on dressing differently than his peers.

4. Playing the ukulele mellifluously and sonorously, Margaret gave an **unparalleled** performance at the Five Star Center for the Performing Arts.

5. Victims of social **alienation** risk becoming mentally and emotionally incapacitated.

# Lesson 13

## Test Takers' Anecdotes

For Kimberly, several sentences in a Humanities passage about Shakespeare were challenging to grasp because of their syntax and vocabulary. One such sentence, for example, read "...after a brief **demurral**, she begins to speak the **enchanting** lines in a **lush** style... different from Bloom's quietly **restrained rendition**." Now that's a mouthful of vocabulary to digest. Grab those index cards!

---

> **bemoans, censor, conjure, demurral, disconcerting**
> **feverish, inevitably, muddled, rendition, supplemented**

---

**bemoans** (v.)   laments, expresses sorrow about something; feels a sense of grief, disappointment, or loss; regret, mourn, complain about something

> Do not **bemoan** the loss of your past; instead, take positive steps every day to create a future filled with the realization of your dreams.

> It is senseless to **bemoan** the loss of material possessions, as they pale in comparison to the unparalleled value of health, security, and emotional well-being.

> Parents and teachers often **bemoan** children's preoccupation with technology at the expense of spending adequate time reading.

**censor** (v.)   to limit content of a movie, publication, play, that is considered offensive; to execute control over a situation that may have the potential to harm others; to edit; to inhibit; to repress

> Snippets of dialogue from the play were **censored** because the directors found the dialogue to be potentially hurtful to the audience.

> To avoid acts of bullying, bystanders should be willing to exert an influence to **censor** the intimidating and spirit-breaking behavior and words of the manipulative bully.

> The managing editor **censored** segments of the newspaper article to paint a more positive picture of the state of affairs surrounding the mayor's office.

**conjure** (v.)   to invoke or summon supernatural forces through incantation or some other acts; to perform magic tricks

> Sofia had her family's home blessed in order to **conjure** benign and beneficial spirits to its doors.

> To **conjure** the spirits of her deceased grandparents, Tatiana scheduled a meeting with an esteemed medium.

> The spiritual guide encouraged her clients to vividly **conjure** up joy and peace-filled visions of their futures since she fully believed that thoughts create reality.

**demurral** (n.)   an objection or avoidance; a refusal; a reluctance; a personal reservation or mild objection

> Both parties embraced the compromise without **demurral**.

> Despite her visible and firm **demurral**, Leo pressed on and insisted that his decision was the only reasonable option.

> Lyrical Laurette, was asked to sing her favorite rap songs and refused; after a short-lived **demurral**, however, she began to recite the lyrics enthusiastically.

**disconcerting** (adj.)   causing an individual to feel uneasy, confused, or disturbed; causing embarrassment or discomfort; upsetting; distressing

> Sandra finds high television volume at night to be **disconcerting**; she needs quiet to fall asleep.

> The tension between Sanjay and his wife was visibly **disconcerting** to those in their company.

> The strident house alarm sounding deafeningly at two in the morning was **disconcerting** for not only the slumbering family but also for the dogs who barked several minutes after!

**feverish** (adj.)   resembling a fever or the intensity characteristic of a fever; restless; marked by intense emotion, interest, or activity; intensely passionate; avid; fervent

> Sheena tidied her son's bedroom at a **feverish** pace, wanting everything perfect and in place; she couldn't wait for his weekend home from college.

> **Feverishly**, Sadie trained as a competitive swimmer, hoping to obtain a college scholarship one day.

> Andre completed his summer assignments **feverishly** so that his time would be freed up for socializing with family and friends.

**inevitability** (adj.)   occurring invariably; unable to be evaded or escaped; certain to or bound to happen; destined to occur; unalterable; predictable

> Don't strangle yourself in a web of lives; **inevitably** all truths reveal themselves.

> **Inevitably**, we mature, self-actualize, and face the truth about the type of person we are: peacemaker or strife maker.

> Though a grim reality to some, growing old is an **inevitable** truth; those who do not reach old age are the unfortunate ones.

**muddled** (adj.)  mixed together in a state of disorder or disarray; relating to a confused or distracted state of thought; characterized as muddy; jumbled; perplexed; bewildered

> Three people talking to her at once **muddled** Gina's train of thought.

> Feeling pulled in too many directions, Cassandra tried to sift through her **muddled** thoughts.

> The institute's line of thought became increasingly **muddled** as too many scientists became involved with the scientific process.

**rendition** (n.)  version or interpretation of a piece of music, drama, or poem, particularly those used in live performance; a translation of some work into another language

> All **renditions** of their wedding song, "All My Life," give her goose bumps and warm nostalgic feelings.

> Nina's **rendition** of the Shakespearean sonnet is the most stirring and sentimental.

> The Italian **rendition** of the ballad is exceptionally soulful and emotionally moving.

**supplemented** (v.)  added to in order to make something more complete or comprehensive; improved, extended, or increased by adding to something in a positive manner

> Lauretta **supplemented** her yoga practice with long beach walks, swimming, and weight training.

> To **supplement** his income earned as a caddie, Ernest is taking on additional responsibilities at the golf club including starter, ranger, and bag room attendant.

> Jolanda **supplemented** her diet with several multivitamins and mineral supplements.

## MEMORY TIPS

Use these mnemonics (memory devices) to boost your vocabulary. Make up your own memory clues for words in this lesson that are personally challenging. Add these tips, and your own, to your Vocabulary Notebook.

### bemoans
If Margo **moans** about how her soufflé collapsed, then she is expressing sadness about something. If your dog **moans** in his sleep, you can imagine he is dreaming about his doggie biscuit treats being depleted.

### disconcerting
People who are in *concert* with one another are in harmonious agreement. Given that the prefix *dis-* means "against," it makes sense that **disconcerting** means "upsetting or lacking in harmony." *Dis-* is also used in *disagreeable, disappearance, dissonance,* and *disassemble.*

### rendition
In a sense, this word has one of its definitions built in: *edition*. A new edition of a song, for example, can come out as a remix, as a dance-tech version, or as an amalgam or amalgamation (a great blend) of a few top songs.

## MATCHING

Match the vocabulary words in Column A with their defining characteristics in Column B.

**Column A**

1. rendition
2. supplement
3. disconcerting
4. bemoans
5. censors

**Column B**

A. one's individual translation or interpretation of a creative work

B. destined to occur; unalterable

C. to add to something to round it off in a positive, comprehensive manner

D. making one feel uncomfortable or uneasy

E. controls or limits something that may be considered harmful

F. to create or come up with something

G. laments; expresses sorrow over a loss

## WORDS IN CONTEXT

Based on the context in which each **bold** word is used, identify the word usage of each sentence as either C (Correct) or I (Incorrect).

1. In Anne's estimation, Andrea Boccelli's **renditions** of love ballads are unparalleled in their soulfulness and tenderness.

2. Witnessing toddlers without life vests frolicking in the tidal wave pool at the water park was **disconcerting** for the safety-conscious mother.

3. **Conjure** an image of the most relaxing and naturally luxuriant vacation spot in the world, and Cabo San Lucas looms panoramically into view!

4. **Feverishly**, the high school students worked through their summer reading assignments at a snail's pace.

5. To **supplement** her husband's income, Gina worked part time as a dental hygienist.

# Lesson 14

## Test Takers' Anecdotes

Mike enjoys reading, sports biographies especially. However, he found parts of the ACT Humanities passages tricky because of the words woven throughout. One sentence in a passage from a book titled *A Field Guide to Wild Flowers*, for example, ended: "the spine grew inevitably **lax**, and some of the margins sprouted **cryptic annotations**." Although the story-line of the passage flowed clearly and logically, the vocabulary dispersed throughout sometimes obscured meaning.

> **annotations, attribute, bog, condescension, cryptic daunting, indispensable, kin, lax, retrospect**

**annotations** (n.)   textual markings and notes; explanatory and critical comments to accompany a text; literary remarks and interpretations

> SAT and ACT tutors are expected to thoroughly **annotate** the reading passages on practice tests before meeting with their students.

> A lover of short stories, Hilde opened her anthology of *Collected Short Works* and read through the myriad **annotations** she had jotted down in the margins of each and every page.

> Rereading *The Great Gatsby* more than twenty years later, Lily nostalgically recalled the abundant **annotations** she had long-ago penned in the margins of the well-worn paperback.

**attribute** (n.)   a characteristic, property, or quality of something or someone

> A true gentleman, Sy is remembered for his many positive **attributes,** which include a soft-spoken demeanor, a jovial personality, and a ready smile.

> Among the university's most appealing **attributes** are a lush and sprawling campus, several large quads, and a new state-of-the-art business building.

> A meal at Moe's Southwest Grill possesses many **attributes** of a delicious dining experience: warm tortillas, delectable guacamole, and zesty salsa!

**bog** (n.)   wet marshland; swampy and soft ground; quagmire

> It rained for four days straight: the Paston's backyard was a veritable **bog**.

> She was invited to go fly fishing with her boyfriend alongside a **bog**; thankfully, she wore her new fatigue-green Hunter boots for this soggy outdoor occasion.

> Imagine a hog wallowing in a mud-soaked **bog**!

**condescension** (n.)   arrogance; pretension; a manner of behavior that shows that an individual thinks he or she is more intelligent or more important than another

> Those who live on a high horse, as the idiom goes, are manipulative purveyors of **condescension**.

> Though Miranda exhibits an icy air of **condescension**, she suffers from low self-esteem and feels ill-equipped in terms of her abilities.

> **Condescendingly**, Connor belittled his girlfriend by repeatedly insisting that she just doesn't understand such complicated matters.

**cryptic** (adj.)   mysterious, puzzling; ambiguous; sometimes relating to secret codes

> A **cryptic** voice mail was left on Pete's cell phone; he could neither determine the caller nor the content of the message.

> **Cryptic** sets of numbers are required to disarm house alarms, open safes, and access online bank accounts.

> When asked to solve the age-old riddle, Joey nodded his head, rubbed his chin and muttered, "Hmmm, **cryptic**."

**daunting** (adj.)   intimidating; tending to frighten or discourage someone; overwhelming

> You will find the writing of the 85,000-word book less **daunting** if you set manageable weekly and monthly goals for word count.

> Sorting through her cluttered closet is a **daunting** task, for it is overloaded with shoes, purses, pants, and outerwear.

> To tackle a **daunting** undertaking, give yourself time to gather your thoughts and then take action: prioritize, act, delegate.

**indispensable** (adj.)   relating to that which is so valuable, useful, or desirable that it cannot be done without; absolutely necessary; vital; essential; unavoidable in terms of having to be addressed and faced

> Trusting, mutually-beneficial relationships are **indispensable** to a person's well-being.

> Committed to staying in shape, Kenzie deemed a brisk walk outdoors or thirty minutes on her elliptical trainer as **indispensable** to her routine.

> The success of their businesses rests on a key premise: the directors view each and every independent contractor as an **indispensable** member of their team.

**kin** (n.)  one's blood relative(s); a member of a group that shares characteristics and traits with another group; one's family connections; kinfolk

> Although Deanne and Jane are not her blood relatives, Cassandra feels as if they are her sisters, her **kin**.

> His wife is deceased, so when Grandpa Lenny passes away his estate will go to his next of **kin**.

> A turtle and a tortoise can be considered **kin** although they're anatomically different, biologically speaking.

**lax** (adj.) not strict, tight, or tense; not stringent; loose, easygoing; relaxed; lenient

> Although Father came across as a martinet, he was actually **lax** when it came to his children's household chores.

> Surprisingly, the coach of the competitive lacrosse club team was quite **lax** about daily practices and drills.

> Dress-down Fridays contribute to the **lax** atmosphere at the congenial office.

**retrospect** (n.)  reflecting on and reviewing past actions in light of new information or with a new perspective

> In **retrospect**, she wished she had spent her junior year abroad in London.

> The adage says, "hindsight is twenty–twenty." In other words, **retrospectively**, we tend to see the past with keenness and clarity of mind.

> **Retrospection** made Rebecca realize that afternoons spent shopping in Soho and strolling South Street Seaport were among her best summer highlights.

## MEMORY TIPS

Use these mnemonics (memory devices) to boost your vocabulary. Make up your own memory clues for words in this lesson that are personally challenging. Add these tips, and your own, to your Vocabulary Notebook.

### bog
Picture this wet, muddy scene: rolling over and splashing around, the *hog* (adult male pig) is delightfully cooling himself off in the chilly *bog*!

### lax
Think re*lax*ed. Or picture a re*lax*ed **lax** coach who is easygoing and jovial, whether or not his team wins the Eastern Seaboard Lacrosse Tournament!

### retrospection
The word roots *spic* and *spec* pertain to seeing and looking, as used in in*spec*t, *spec*tacle, or *spec*tate. The prefix *retro-* means prior or early. Piece these word parts together to get a working definition of **retrospection**: "seeing the prior picture." Just as hindsight is twenty-twenty, so oftentimes **retrospection** is twenty-twenty, as well.

## MATCHING

Match the vocabulary words in Column A with their defining characteristics in Column B.

**Column A**

1. bog
2. kin
3. attribute
4. retrospect
5. daunting

**Column B**

A. intimidating, overwhelming

B. a defining characteristic or quality; trait

C. mysterious and puzzling

D. reflecting on past events, actions

E. family relations; relatives

F. a collection of short works of fiction

G. a swamp or marshland

## WORDS IN CONTEXT

Based on the context in which each **bold** word is used, identify the word usage of each sentence as either C (Correct) or I (Incorrect).

1. Two of his best **attributes** are his can-do attitude and his relaxed demeanor.

2. **Lax** parenting may lead to undisciplined children.

3. Fresh air and exercise are **indispensable** to an unhealthy lifestyle.

4. The marshy **bog** in the corner of the backyard is surrounded by large round stones; when it rains, it fills up with water and looks more like a pond than a **bog**.

5. In the margins of the dining guide are scribbled **annotations**, commenting widely on the best appetizers, entrées, and desserts.

# Lesson 15

## Test Takers' Anecdotes

For Harriet, a Humanities passage about Indian-inspired music in New York became very challenging when she encountered the following words among the answer choices to the reading questions: **premiere**, **scorn**, **indifference**. In the passage itself, she grappled with challenging words such as **eclecticism**, **rendezvous**, and **recapitulate**, among others.

Tom read a Humanities passage about French philosopher and mathematician, Descartes. He couldn't seem to fully absorb the descriptive comments about the narrator's background because some phrases had within them words with which Tom did not feel completely comfortable. Such phrases included "academically **disinclined** background" and "not materially **deprived**." The ten corresponding questions and their answer choices contained additional challenging words, including **rudimentary**, **inevitably**, **metaphysical**, **chronological**, and **fleeting**.

---

**connote, eclecticism, fusions, improvisers, labyrinthine,
mutiny, premiere, punctuate, recapitulate, rendezvous**

---

**connote** (v.)   to suggest or imply something beyond its original or literal meaning

His hesitancy to make decisions **connotes** his irresolute nature.

The term *ski lodge* **connotes** warmth, coziness, gathering with family and friends, and a mug brimming with hot cocoa.

The soul stirring music and lyrics of the word renowned tenor **connotes** lifelong devotion and romance.

**eclecticism** (n.)   something of particular interest because it is comprised of many different things, styles, and tastes

> Sheila has an **eclectic** palate and enjoys foods across the culinary gamut: sushi, caviar, and pigs-in-blankets!

> The college suite décor shows **eclecticism**: each resident's belongings exhibit a distinctive style ranging from contemporary sleek to country chic.

> She effectively uses a dynamic, **eclectic** approach to teaching that includes rote recall and reinforcement, mnemonic devices, and personal connections to new information.

**fusions** (n.)   the merging or blending of two or more styles, materials, or ideas; blends, hybrids, combinations; the composition of musical elements or styles into a single musical rendition; the molten state of a substance

> Asian **Fusion** is one of the family's favorite new local restaurants because of its tasty blends, or **fusions**, of the flavors of Japanese, Chinese, and Thai cuisine.

> Howard's garden fresh herbs—cilantro, parsley, and basil—created a delectable **fusion** of flavors.

> The aromatherapy perfume is composed of a **fusion** of essential oils.

**improvisers** (n.)   individuals who spontaneously create art, music, or drama; performers who make up or create a play, a song, or musical composition on the spot in an unrehearsed manner

> Some of the best chefs are master **improvisers** in the kitchen, as they incorporate herbs, flavors, and spices in unique combinations.

> People who prefer to play the day by ear and see how the hours unfold tend to be **improvisers** rather than planners.

> The Summer Stage Theater prided itself on its off-the-cuff, freshly **improvised** performances.

**labyrinthine** (adj.)   of, like, or resembling a maze or labyrinth; intricate, complex, tangled

> The rugged path through the nature preserve was **labyrinthine**; walkers, hikers, and cyclists could choose from one of several winding ways through the wooded trail.

> Some mathematical processes are so **labyrinthine** that they feel more like mazes than calculations.

> Jake's mode of thinking is so disconnected and scattered that he habitually creates a **labyrinthine** process out of a simple set of steps.

**mutiny** (n.)   a rebellion against authority, particularly that of soldiers refusing to obey orders as given by their commanding officers; an uprising; an insurgence

> The sailors covertly planned a **mutiny** against their captain, whom they regarded as incompetent as well as cruel.

> In April of 1789, **mutiny** occurred on the *Bounty*, the British Royal Navy ship called *Bounty*.

> Unanimously, the naval crew decided to carry out a **mutiny** against their superiors.

**premiere** (adj.)   relating to the first performance or showing of a play or movie, for instance, through a public venue; the first in importance; debut; opening (v.) to show or broadcast a movie or play for the first time

> Her **premiere** book discussion took place at the Barnes and Noble bookstore in Manhasset, New York.

> Andre's **premiere** oral presentation took place at the Long Island Math Fair, which was held at Hofstra University.

> Complete with little known recipes and mouth-watering photos, the regional Italian cookbook **premieres** next fall.

**punctuate** (v.) to stress, highlight, accentuate, or emphasize

> To **punctuate** his exotic travel journals, Richard includes riveting dialogue and descriptions that are, at once, both witty and vivid.

> Existing among ceaseless activity and din served to **punctuate** the peacefulness of a brief escape to the quietude of her room.

> To **punctuate** the delectable taste of the country-style pork ribs, Mrs. Benz slathered them in Sweet Baby Ray's honey barbecue sauce before tossing them onto the hot grill.

**recapitulate** (v.) to summarize; to review; to reiterate or recap; to provide a synopsis of something

> In detail, **recapitulate** the topics covered during your one-on-one mentoring session.

> "**Recapitulate** for me and Detective Smith," the officer stated, "the events of that morning."

> Please **recapitulate** the topics covered during your chemistry lab this afternoon.

**rendezvous** (n.) a popular location for people to meet and gather; a secret meeting arranged, usually between lovers; a tryst; an appointment

> The couple's favorite meeting place for their weekly **rendezvous** was a weather-worn bench overlooking the harbor in the whaling town of Port Harrison.

> Their Friday night **rendezvous** was set for one of their favorite places, the boardwalk at the nearby Sunset Beach.

> Their Friday night get-togethers to listen to live music at the beach bandstand were weekend **rendezvous** they all looked forward to.

## MEMORY TIPS

Use these mnemonics (memory devices) to boost your vocabulary. Make up your own memory clues for words in this lesson that are personally challenging. Add these tips, and your own, to your Vocabulary Notebook.

### <u>pre</u>miere

The commonly used prefix *pre-* means "before" and sometimes can be used to mean "first," "prior," "preliminary," or "early." Think of this prefix's usage in words such as: *pre*amble, *pre*school, *pre*arranged, *pre*maturity, and *pre*cooked. So the ***premiere*** showing of the play is the first in line, the first performance of its kind.

### punctuate

Think about how punctuation marks such as the question mark (?) and the exclamation point (!) stress or accentuate the tone and meaning of a sentence.

## MATCHING

Match the vocabulary words in Column A with their defining characteristics in Column B.

**Column A**

1. recapitulate
2. rendezvous
3. labyrinthine
4. connote
5. fusions

**Column B**

A. to suggest the meaning of something

B. a secret meeting; tryst

C. the first showing; the debut

D. mazelike; convoluted; intricate

E. to run through and summarize

F. blends of tastes, styles

G. taken from various sources

## WORDS IN CONTEXT

Based on the context in which each **bold** word is used, identify the word usage of each sentence as either C (Correct) or I (Incorrect).

1. Sheena decorated strictly with country French furnishings and accessories; her style was as far from **eclectic** as interior décor can be.

2. To **punctuate** the flavor of the thinly sliced chicken breasts, Cynthia added fresh rosemary, lemon, and a few sprinkles of turmeric.

3. Regardless of his efforts to consult a paper map, use Google map, and plug his destination into his navigation system, the route to the ski house still seemed perplexing and **labyrinthine**.

4. Cultural **fusions** can be enlightening and enriching, as aspects of each way of life are merged, creating a unique perspective.

5. The members of the **improvisational** theater group rehearsed daily for months before opening night.

# Part IV
# Reading Test:
# Natural Science Vocabulary

Topics addressed in this category include anatomy, astronomy, biology, botany, chemistry, ecology, medicine, meteorology, microbiology, natural history, physiology, physics, technology, and zoology.

## Word Bank

The words below are from the Natural Science section of ACT practice exams. These words have all presented some level of difficulty, confusion, or uncertainty for students. This comprehensive list includes words from the passages themselves, from the questions, and from the answer choices. Not every word in this vocabulary bank is included in the following lessons, which feature only ten words each. Only those words that tend to appear most frequently on exams or those that students found the most unclear are examined in depth.

## Natural Science Reading Passages

Words listed appear within the passages and/or their corresponding questions. **Test 1**: agility, cohesiveness, correlation, criterion, demise, depict, flawed, interstices, longevity, obtuseness, paragons, periphery, preconceived, proposition, prowess, quintessential, solace, subjective, torrent; **Test 2**: acutely, aesthetic, anomalies, anthropologist, contemporaries, correlates, dismissed, flux, fused, illuminant, inquiry, limbo, mediocre, opus, preoccupation, notion, skepticism, whimsy; **Test 3**: apocalypse, channels, contending, derived, dowry, irreconcilable, plume, prevailed, prevalent, projectile, speculated, succession, terrestrial, uncannily, vaporizes; **Test 4**: acute, attributes, chamber, colleague, entails, evaluative, extract, facets, gauge, incubation, metamorphosed, septillion, specimen, vital; **Test 5**: allegedly, apparent, appendages, atop, bizarre, census, contend, disintegrating, documents, ecosystem, encompasses, essentially, incidentally, indistinguishably, lurking, marine, minuscule, proximity, remote, remotely, skepticism, specimens, stance, submersibles, tendrilous, tizzy, undetected, unintentionally, verified.

# Lesson 16

## Test Takers' Anecdotes

On a Natural Science passage about German philosopher Vincent van Goethe's color theory, Grant erroneously chose **skepticism** as his answer to a question about another philosopher's expression of *attitude* toward Goethe's theory. Once I defined the word **skepticism** for him, as meaning "uncertain" or "doubtful," Grant immediately knew it wasn't the right choice and picked the correct answer, which was *respect*.

Eels are the topic of a natural science passage that appeared on a real and recently released ACT. Trevor had some trouble fully absorbing the characteristics of the eels, as he encountered several unfamiliar words in the descriptions of these creatures. These words included: "**invariably** wind up in European rivers," "feed **voraciously** and change color," and "their digestive systems will **atrophy**." In addition, Trevor lacked clarity on the meanings of **osmosis**, **brackish**, and **estuaries**, which were used within the paragraphs of this Natural Science reading passage.

---

agility, cohesiveness, correlation, demise, longevity
paragon, preconceived, prowess, quintessential, subjective

---

**agility** (n.)   nimbleness and flexibility in body and mind, limberness; litheness; ability to move with ease and grace

> To prepare for baseball season, he attended speed and **agility** training during his winter off-season.

> Ten years of soccer training enhanced Phil's **agility** across all sports pursuits, including downhill skiing and skim boarding.

> Given her remarkable mental **agility**, Andrea was also able to make sophisticated mathematical calculations in her mind with outstanding accuracy.

**cohesiveness** (n.)   the quality of working together as a unified whole; effectively coming together to form a strong and organized unit

> The **cohesiveness** of the attorney's succinct and logical argument won his client's case.

> In order to write a **cohesive** essay, the author should build logically upon his general lines of reasoning, use specific illustrative examples, and use transitional language effectively.

> Pink, white, and black is the color scheme of Melissa's dorm room; in fact, her black-and-white desk accessories match both aesthetically and **cohesively**.

**correlation** (n.)   a correspondence or necessary relationship; an association of ideas, dynamics, or individual units

> Social researches have repeatedly demonstrated that there exists a striking **correlation** between poverty and crime.

> "A direct **correlation** exists between a sluggish body and a sluggish mind," commented Professor Douglas emphatically.

> Is there a real **correlation** between stress and weight gain?

**demise** (n.)   death; decay; destruction; deterioration; gradual decline

> The esteemed leader's **demise** caused unrest and despondency among the citizens of the province.

> The **demise** of the company was caused by miscommunication and breached loyalties.

> Most unfortunate was the **demise** of the Mandarin program, as eliminating any languages from the foreign language department is always a significant loss.

**longevity** (n.)   long life; duration of one's life span

> To increase our **longevity**, we should eat natural and whole foods, exercise regularly, and maintain balance in our personal, social, and spiritual lives.

> An elephant's **longevity** is somewhere between sixty and seventy years.

> An indirect relationship exists between an individual's stress level and his or her **longevity**.

**paragon** (n.)   someone or something that is the very best model or example; a prime example; archetype

> Lucy is a **paragon** of politeness, while Bruce is an archetype of abrasiveness and curtness.

> An esteemed **paragon** of fairness and good will, the high school teacher offers extra help every day after school, allows rewrites on term papers, and drops each student's lowest quiz grade.

> Striving to be **paragons** was counterproductive for the women. As their true and fallible selves were unknown to others, authentic friendships could not be formed.

**preconceived** (adj.)   formulated, in advance, in the mind prior to one's gathering adequate information; reflecting an individual's personal prejudices, without forming one's opinions based on real life experience and interaction; predetermined; fixed; rigid

> To cultivate an open mind, one should let go of his or her **preconceived** ideas about how business, politics, or marriage should be.

> Toss your **preconceived** notions to the curb, and nurture in yourself a receptive heart and mind.

> **Preconceived** biases often change as one immerses oneself in the day-to-day realities of the world.

**prowess** (n.)   noteworthy, distinguished valor; skill and bravery, especially as that displayed in the military as; extraordinary ability

> Six-pack Sergio is well known for his **prowess** in the boxing ring.

> Pete's **prowess** in training animals is remarkable; he even got Wayward Willy to roll over and play dead!

> Both their military and air force **prowess** are impressive.

**quintessential** (adj.)   a thing's true, primary essence in its purest and most concentrated form; the most typical, representative expression or example of something

> Patient, nurturing, and attentive, Cynthia is the **quintessential** mother.

> The Deluxe Dragon Roll was voted to be the **quintessence** of the perfectly designed brown rice sushi roll.

> A selfless nature to serve others is the **quintessential** expression of kindness and charity.

**subjective** (adj.)   based on opinions, personal bias

> What makes a college appealing is truly **subjective**. One high school senior might be drawn to a scenic, country campus, the other to a frenetic urban center.

> Additional components of a great college experience are also **subjective**. For some it's the availability of internships, for others it's the party scene.

> **Subjective** assessments are based on opinions and subtleties instead of the numbers and data of objective analyses.

## MEMORY TIPS

Use these mnemonics (memory devices) to boost your vocabulary. Make up your own memory clues for words in this lesson that are personally challenging. Add these tips, and your own, to your Vocabulary Notebook.

### longevity

To harness the meaning of this word in a nutshell, think "long life." As you recall, *longevity* refers to the life span of a person or animal as well as the span of one's career.

### prowess

Scramble the letters in **prowess** to get *powers*! As we can think of *powers* as great skills and abilities, the word *powers* provides a helpful link to the meaning of **prowess**.

### subjective

A *subject* is the person being written about, spoken about, or referred to. For example, the subject of a biography might be Eleanor Roosevelt or Lance Armstrong. Given that a subject is an individual, think of how **subjective** points of view are those based on an individual subject's opinions and points of view.

## MATCHING

Match the vocabulary words in Column A with their defining characteristics in Column B.

| Column A | Column B |
|---|---|
| 1. prowess | A. a correspondence in relationship |
| 2. demise | B. skill or ability attributed to an individual |
| 3. subjective | C. destruction, decay, and death |
| 4. paragon | D. a model of excellence; paradigm |
| 5. agility | E. ease or grace in movement; nimbleness |
|  | F. the life span of a species |
|  | G. based on bias and opinion |

## WORDS IN CONTEXT

Based on the context in which each **bold** word is used, identify the word usage of each sentence as either C (Correct) or I (Incorrect).

1. Raj's **mental** agility is evident, for he can solve intricate quadratic equations in his head in under a minute!

2. Pia is a **paragon** of peace; she sees, hears, and speaks well of all with whom she comes in contact.

3. To promote the health and **longevity** of her loved ones, Cassie prepares organic produce, fish, and a whole grain such as barley for her family several days per week.

4. The **cohesiveness** of the courtroom litigator's argument made him lose the case.

5. Job loss and homelessness have resulted from the **demise** of the once thriving city.

# Lesson 17

## Test Takers' Anecdotes

After just the first two sentences of a natural science passage about color theory, Kevin's line of thought was distracted by several words used in these opening sentences alone: **opus**, **dismissed**, **contemporaries**, **limbo**, **whimsy**, **pseudoscience**, **anomalies**, and **fluctuations**. Had he been more solid on the meanings of these words, his comprehension would have been that much stronger and accurate.

---

> **anomalies, anthropologist, contemporaries, dismissed**
>
> **flux, illuminant, inquiry, limbo, opus, preoccupation**

---

**anomalies** (n.)   individuals, things, or occurrences that deviate from the norm or differ from expectations; someone or something difficult to name, define, or classify; unusual or unexpected entities; peculiarities; abnormalities rarities

> In a family in which living the good life takes all priority, those who reach out to help others are the **anomalies**.

> Though she felt sluggish and ill, the doctors could not find any **anomalies** in her blood work or other testing.

> The meat and potato eaters are the **anomalies** among those who feast voraciously on fish, fowl, and greens.

**anthropologist** (n.)  an individual who studies humankind in all its aspects, especially human culture or human development

> The studies of an **anthropologist** differ from those of a sociologist because the latter takes a more integrated historical and comparative approach to his discipline.

> Behavioral ecologists and **anthropologists** profoundly complement and edify each other's research.

> Among the dream destinations of the academic **anthropologist** are Egypt, Jerusalem, and Greece.

**contemporaries** (n.)  people who are the same or approximately the same age; one's peers or colleagues

> With their **contemporaries**, the teen boys liked to play cards, play basketball, and watch movies.

> More often than not, people have the most in common with their **contemporaries**.

> Although they are **contemporaries** living in the same neighborhood, the forty-somethings had little in common.

**dismissed** (v.)  pushed aside, ignored; rejected or refused to give something or someone consideration; stopped someone's term of employment

> Although she clearly and thoroughly expressed her point of view, it was quickly **dismissed** by those who felt they know best.

> She was **dismissed** from the office not because she wasn't qualified but because she was downright snooty.

> The preschoolers are promptly **dismissed** from school at 2:40 in the afternoon.

**flux** (n.)   instability; a dynamic of constant change; vacillation, wavering

> Although most people desire security and stability, continual **flux** perseveres as the fundamental nature of human existence.

> Frequently changing interest rates indicate that the economy is in a state of **flux**.

> "Nothing in this world is permanent but change," Lizbeth asserted mindfully. "In other words," she continued, "Life's only constant is **flux**."

**illuminant** (n.)   something that provides light or that gives off light; a source of light

> Shining bright and white in the night sky, the moon is our great celestial **illuminant**.

> We used the reflection of light from the patio lanterns as our evening **illuminant** in order to play our final round of canasta at the patio table.

> In case of a blackout, the couple kept their home well stocked with battery operated lanterns, large pillar candles, flashlights, and other emergency **illuminants**.

**inquiry** (n.)   a series of questions; the process of asking in order to gather information or to determine the facts of a given situation or case; an investigation; an examination or survey

> The process of scientific **inquiry** often starts with a hypothesis, which is otherwise known as a tentative premise or theory.

> A conversation with Mia was less of a pleasant exchange of information back and forth, and more of an incessant **inquiry** directed at the person to whom she repeatedly questioned.

> Amazed by Grace's volleyball skills, Monica **inquired** about her sports involvement in high school and college.

**limbo** (n.)   a state of waiting and uncertainty; a state of oblivion; an indeterminate state of being

> Undecided whether to live at home or go away to college, Henrietta lived a student's life in **limbo**.

> For Natasha, living in a state of **limbo** was very challenging, as she couldn't plan for the changes that would have to take place.

> Undecided whether to become a biomedical research scientist or a medical doctor, Troy found himself in a career **limbo** that lasted for about a year.

**opus** (n.)   any great work of art, particularly a musical work or series created by an accomplished composer; a great work of literature; magnum opus; composition

> *Mr. Holland's* **Opus** is a touching 1995 movie that chronicles and dramatizes the life of a high school music teacher and his impact on those around him.

> It took the author two years to write, revise, and edit her **opus**, which consisted of thirty-five chapters and 55,000 words.

> The SoHo artist's **opus**, a riveting amalgam of scrap metal, concrete, and recycled water bottles, was displayed in Washington Square Park.

**preoccupation** (n.)   a state of being overly concerned with or focused on something, someone, or some situation; a fixation or obsession

> Despite his **preoccupation** with physical appearances, Miguel, surprisingly, is a man of considerable depth and exhibits great sensitivity and compassion for others.

> Juliet's **preoccupation** with herself is apparent in how she spends her time and money.

> **Preoccupation** with just about anything or anyone is undesirable, as balance is the key to living a complete life.

## MEMORY TIPS

Use these mnemonics (memory devices) to boost your vocabulary. Make up your own memory clues for words in this lesson that are personally challenging. Add these tips, and your own, to your Vocabulary Notebook.

### illuminant
Picture a beautiful <u>lumina</u>ry, such as white bags filled with candles lining the walkway to a home, welcoming you to a soirée (an evening get-together). Envision lily-shaped luminaries floating in a backyard pool in the evening, giving off enough light to toast s'mores in a fire pit.

### opus
A simple definition for **opus** is a *work*, as in a work of art. Usually, an *opus* refers to a musical work or composition. Simply connect this four-letter definition (w-o-r-k) with the four-letter vocabulary word, o-p-u-s. As easy as 1-2-3-4.

## MATCHING

Match the vocabulary words in Column A with their defining characteristics in Column B.

| Column A | Column B |
| --- | --- |
| 1. flux | A. a question or investigation |
| 2. limbo | B. rarities; unusual elements |
| 3. contemporaries | C. a state of uncertainty; an indeterminate state or midpoint |
| 4. inquiry | D. a great worry or obsession |
| 5. anomalies | E. a state of dynamic fluctuation |
|  | F. something that gives off or reflects light |
|  | G. people who are similar in age or of the same generation |

## WORDS IN CONTEXT

Based on the context in which each **bold** word is used, identify the word usage of each sentence as either C (Correct) or I (Incorrect).

1. Undecided whether to attend a city or rural campus, Jim found himself in a state of **limbo** when it came to applying to college.

2. In a family of physical fitness enthusiasts, couch potato Ian is the **anomaly**.

3. The Jones family used soup bowls as **illuminants** during the hurricane.

4. Wearing the same boots and coats from ten years ago, Kendra exhibits a **preoccupation** with fashion trends.

5. Are they selling their home or staying put? The vacillating DiFrancos were in a state of **flux** for several months.

# Lesson 18

## Test Takers' Anecdotes

On the April 2013 real ACT, the Natural Science passage is about string theory and the unifying laws of physics. In the first and second body paragraphs alone, Vanessa encountered a host of potentially challenging words that appear. Ask yourself: *How comfortable would I be if I were to encounter the following group of words in just two of the nine paragraphs that make up the passage? How fluent would my reading and understanding be?* Would words like these be comfortable for you, or would they be obstacles, as they were for Vanessa? Here they are: **envisage**, **elongating**, **coils**, **impenetrable**, **elite**, **vexing**, **deficit**, **realms**, **quantum**, **rectify**, **notions**, **myriad**, **interface**, and **multiplicity**.

> **apocalypse, contending, irreconcilable, plume, prevalent projectile, succession, terrestrial, uncannily, vaporizes**

---

**apocalypse** (n.) a situation characterized by great destruction, devastation, and death; a revelation pertaining to the future of the world; the time of the world's destruction; catastrophe

Instead of expecting positive change, Winona pictures an **apocalypse** during which everything that could go wrong does.

Tornados, hurricanes, tsunamis—one natural disaster after the next made it seem that a global scale **apocalypse** was imminent.

Instead of conjuring up mental images of **apocalyptic** events, focus your energy on positive images of a healthful, peaceful, and prosperous future.

**contending** (adj.)   battling for power, influence, authority, or control; competing, rivaling

> **Contending** theories resulted from the three-hour biology lab study, inspiring new inquiries and experiments.

> Hannah and Hank are in a perpetual power struggle, as each **contends** for authority and "the last word" in their tumultuous household.

> Once cooperative and peaceable friends, Gus and Gary are now **contending** rivals who inexorably try to manipulate and one-up the other.

**irreconcilable** (adj.)   unable to smooth over differences with another person, entity, or organization; unwilling to compromise or yield to another or to something else; incompatible; implacable; conflicting

> Despite their **irreconcilable** differences in perspective, Ms. Jones and Ms. Gaving remain civil to each other.

> Superstring theory attempts to bring together the long **contending** theories of general relativity and quantum mechanics.

> To a peacemaker, no feud or difference of opinion is beyond **irreconcilable** when each party puts forth honesty and good will.

**plume** (n.)   a large feather, sometimes used for decorative purposes; a rising, cylindrical shape of something such as dust, smoke, or water; a cloud or upward spiral

> The **plume** of smoke gradually expanded as more and more gases filtered out of the factory's smokestack.

> The volcanic ash and lava erupted over the mountain, forming an expansive **plume** that lit up the night sky.

> The tribe's chief wore a colorful and lavish **plume** on his headdress as a symbol of his rank and honor.

**prevalent** (adj.) widespread, pervasive, prevailing; present all over; ubiquitous

Which toxins are most **prevalent** in the atmospheres of major cities?

The doctor of optometry explained the most **prevalent** diseases of the human eye.

Fashion-minded Farrah inquired, "Which designer logos are most **prevalent** at the off-campus fraternity mixers: Ralph Lauren Polo, American Eagle, or Lacoste?"

**projectile** (n.) an object propelled forward in space; a fired, launched, or thrown object; a missile

Electron accelerator chambers use subatomic parts as **projectiles** traveling at the speed of light in grand experiments designed to investigate the formation of the universe.

The cement **projectile** flew out of the pickup truck and onto her windshield, leaving a crack the size of a quarter!

For three-year-old Tristan, most household items could be used as **projectiles**, including pistachios, plums, and bagels!

**succession** (n.) a sequence of things, people, or events happening one after the other; following; a progression

The science fiction movie vividly depicted how, in **succession**, the meteors pelted the planet's surface, leading to a mammoth and fiery explosion.

For three days in **succession**, a lack of rainwater exacerbated the present drought.

Ecological **succession** is the study, over an extended period of time, of the observed processes of change in the various species living within a given ecological community.

**terrestrial** (adj.)   of or relating to the earth and land; pertaining to the soil, the ground, the earth

> Although some dream of space travel, others wish to behold the **terrestrial** wonders of our world such as the Grand Canyon, the Redwood Forests, and Niagara Falls.

> Because she would typically become seasick on a sailboat or speedboat, the landlubber declared herself a veritable **terrestrial** creature.

> Kira favors **terrestrial** beings such as rabbits and chipmunks over water dwellers such as eels and koi fish.

**uncannily** (adv.)   strangely, eerily, extraordinarily; seeming to be supernaturally based

> **Uncannily**, nosy Nellie knew the family's schedule and commitments for each upcoming weekend.

> Although he had no indication of the award, he predicted, **uncannily**, to the dollar how much he would be awarded by the scholarship fund.

> The clairvoyant was able to **uncannily** identify each participant's spiritual struggle to such a fine degree of accuracy that she turned all the skeptics into believers.

**vaporizes** (v.)   changes or converts into a vapor; to dissolve a solid into smoke or gas

> When Mentos are dropped into a bottle of seltzer water, the white round mints **vaporize** as gaseous bubbles start rising to the top.

> Like a classic Star Trek adventurer, Kurt disappears so abruptly from a room that he seems to **vaporize** out of sight!

> At the Halloween party, dry ice eerily **vaporized** from a black witch's cauldron, which was set at the center of the buffet.

## MEMORY TIPS

Use these mnemonics (memory devices) to boost your vocabulary. Make up your own memory clues for words in this lesson that are personally challenging. Add these tips, and your own, to your Vocabulary Notebook.

### terrestrial

The word root *terra* relates to and signifies "dry land, earth, soil, and the ground." Consider its use in common words such as *terrain, territory,* and *terra-cotta.*

### vaporizes

Visualize how the Star Trek characters vaporize as they stand on their platform and travel from one place to another. In this scientific world, their bodies turn to *vapor* (steam, mist) as they are transported to a new location.

## MATCHING

Match the vocabulary words in Column A with their defining characteristics in Column B.

**Column A**

1. terrestrial
2. plume
3. apocalypse
4. uncannily
5. projectile

**Column B**

A. something that follows a trajectory or path of movement

B. fighting against one another; competing; vying

C. relating to the land, soil, and earth

D. the end of the Earth; end of days

E. oddly, strangely

F. a large cloud of smoke, dust, gas

G. a progression or sequence of things

## WORDS IN CONTEXT

Based on the context in which each **bold** word is used, identify the word usage of each sentence as either C (Correct) or I (Incorrect).

1. Substances that **vaporize** materialize into concrete form.

2. An **apocalyptic** series of events can mark a new age, a time of peace and positive transformation.

3. **Uncannily**, Connor is able to close his eyes and accurately indicate the images his friend, seated in a closed-off room several feet away, has sketched on a set of index cards.

4. In the family's fantasy football league, the whimsical names of **contending** teams include Hurricane Luca, Leapfrog, and Carney Ville!

5. On and off campus, the university's name and logo are **prevalent** on students' clothing, exhibiting the students' pride in their school.

# Lesson 19

## Test Takers' Anecdotes

Isiah normally finds the Natural Science passages interesting. The April 2013 ACT, however, had a somewhat complicated passage on string theory. Ian decided to read the closing paragraph of this cerebral physics passage with particular attention, but found several words in the mix a bit tricky in context, including: **advocates**, **rebuttal**, **humble**, **complacent**, and **ossified**. On the very first question, he hit three words on which he wasn't completely clear: **entrenched**, **prominent**, and **supplant**. He wouldn't call these words roadblocks; nonetheless, his being uncertain about their meanings made the question that much harder.

---

> **colleagues, evaluative, extract, facets, gauge**
> **incubation, metamorphosed, septillion, specimen, vital**

---

**colleagues** (n.)   individuals who work together; coworkers, particularly those in a skilled job or profession; fellow workers

> Dr. Detrick and his **colleagues** are attending their annual medical conference in Denver.

> Physician's assistants, nurses, and lab technologists are among Dr. Rodriguez's **colleagues** at Downtown Hospital.

> This summer, the teachers attending a training workshop that focused on using graphic organizers in note-taking; the seminar was led by one of their **colleagues**, Adjunct Professor of English, Anna Clemmens.

**evaluative** (adj.)   pertaining to the assessment of the value, the importance, or quality of something; based on examination and judgment

> Skill-building drills, monthly diagnostic tests, and other **evaluative** assessments are recommended by the tutoring company.

> **Evaluative** quarterly projects may include research papers, oral presentations, or PowerPoint presentations.

> Seeking to improve future programs, the biology professor asked his students to write **evaluative** assessments of their experiences during their winter study session in the Florida Keys.

**extract** (v.)   to pull something out using force; to obtain something from its source by separating it from material that surrounds it; to copy a passage from a text; to derive pleasure from something; (n.)   an excerpt from a movie script or passage; a concentrated and purified substance or solution

> When reading long critical reading passages, it is wise to first **extract** the main idea from the introductory material or preface.

> Hilde adds pure, all-natural vanilla **extract** to her berry-filled baked oatmeal.

> Tiffany **extracts** strength, limberness, lucidity, and spiritual centeredness from her yoga practice.

**facets** (n.)   aspects, features, or parts of something; the flat surfaces of a cut gemstone; factors, components

> The finely polished flat surfaces of her solitaire diamond, otherwise known as **facets**, glimmered in the sun.

> The Waterford crystal desk clock was shaped like a diamond; its finely honed **facets** caught the light of the chandelier, reflecting rainbows on the living room walls.

> Her leadership style is an effective and estimable blend of several admirable **facets**.

**gauge** (v.)   to measure or estimate; to determine the size, amount, or development of something; to formulate an evaluative judgment of something that is changeable and uncertain; to assess

How do you **gauge** the level of your success?

Because myriad intangible factors are involved, it is difficult to **gauge** the stress level of an individual.

To **gauge** an individual student's academic progress, a variety of assessment tools can be used.

**incubation** (n.)   the period of time between exposure to a pathogen, chemical, or radiation and the point at which symptoms of illness first become evident or detected; the phase and time lapse in the development of disease between infection and manifest symptoms

From conception to **incubation** to birth, the baby chicks were cared for by the first graders and their parents; all the while the children drew and wrote in their journals about the chicks' gradual development.

In a slow process of **incubation**, the tumor cells eventually lodged in the patient's liver.

According to the United States government's Centers for Disease Control, the typical **incubation** period for the influenza virus is one to four days on average.

**metamorphosed** (v.)   changed, transformed, developed from one physical form or structure to another; to change character, condition, or appearance; to undergo bodily changes during growth; mutated; altered; transmuted; morphed

After months of weight training religiously, Emily was gradually able to have some of her fat cells **metamorphose** into lean muscle.

Over the course of a few days, the swallow **metamorphosed** from a debilitated, panting bird to one that flew off like a champ!

Before their eyes, the lizard **metamorphosed** into a fire-breathing dragon!

**septillion** (n.)   the number created when the digit "1" is followed by twenty-four zeros; a trillion trillion; the number ten to the twenty-forth power

> "For the **septillionth** time," Mother pleaded with exasperation, "please put up a load of your laundry."

> One can hardly fathom the number of grains of sand on the ocean shores; suffice to say, there must be **septillion**!

> Filling up several tall glass vases with shiny brown acorns, the inquisitive and energetic child seemed to collect nearly a **septillion** of these brown nuggets from the tree-lined court in front of his home.

**specimen** (n.)   a sample or representative thing or unit; a sample used for diagnostic testing; a type of person who exhibits a particular set of characteristics; an example; a sample; a sampling

> A **specimen** of the eye tumor was sent to the lab for diagnostic testing.

> Part of the hiring process involved a handwriting **specimen**, which was used to analyze the employment candidate's personality.

> Miranda is a repugnant **specimen** of excessive self-indulgence.

**vital** (adj.)   necessary for the survival of something or some population; necessary to maintaining the effectiveness of something or some organization; critical; indispensable; relating to life, the need for life and vitality; very important; imperative; essential

> Eating at least five servings of fruits and vegetables each day is **vital** to a person's health.

> **Vital** to Valerie's emotional and mental well-being is time alone to be quiet, to think, and to just be.

> Walking back and forth to her place of work and working on her feet until her late eighties, Laura remained **vital**, animated, and independent, until her peaceful passing at home at the age of ninety-three.

## MEMORY TIPS

Use these mnemonics (memory devices) to boost your vocabulary. Make up your own memory clues for words in this lesson that are personally challenging. Add these tips, and your own, to your Vocabulary Notebook.

**colleagues**
Picture the word *colleges* embedded within this word. Think of one's **colleagues** at *college* being one's classmates and peers.

**extract**
Let the prefix *ex-* (which means "out," "out of," or "from") remind you that **extract** means to "take something *out*, usually by force." Consider the appearance of *ex-* in *expunge, expel,* and *expurgate.*

## MATCHING

Match the vocabulary words in Column A with their defining characteristics in Column B.

**Column A**

1. vital
2. colleagues
3. extract
4. gauge
5. specimen

**Column B**

A. to measure or estimate

B. a sample or sampling of something

C. to pull something out, usually by using force

D. indispensable; necessary

E. aspects, parts, or features of some whole

F. changed form; transformed physically

G. coworkers

## WORDS IN CONTEXT

Based on the context in which each **bold** word is used, identify the word usage of each sentence as either C (Correct) or I (Incorrect).

1. Over time, Tyrone **metamorphosed** from a type-A, power-driven personality into a laid-back, self-assured individual.

2. The short **incubation** period of the virus made curbing its spread exceedingly difficult.

3. **Vital** to one's physical and emotional well-being are quality foods, daily vitamin supplements, and adequate sleep, rest, and relaxation.

4. There are many **facets** of his personality that attract Lisa, including his street smarts, tenderness, and devotion to his family.

5. The endodontic surgeon showed his patient a **specimen** of the molar root he was fabricating for her from a biocompatible latex-like material, gutta-percha, which is derived from the bark of tropical trees native to Southeast Asia.

# Lesson 20

## Test Takers' Anecdotes

A few nights ago, Kayla remarked how a fairly interesting Natural Science passage (about the life cycle and the living habits of squids) was particularly hard. In just *one* sentence, Kayla faced this fairly challenging vocabulary obstacle course: **stance**, **apparent**, **proximity**, **submersibles**.

---

> **apparent, census, documents, ecosystem, encompasses**
> **indistinguishable, minuscule, stance, submersibles, tendrilous**

---

**apparent** (adj.)  obvious; easily seen or understood; transparent

Based on all she says and does, Leslie has a warm, jovial, and benevolent personality that is readily **apparent**.

Given their spending habits, a robust financial cushion is **apparent**.

**Apparently**, Bruce's bark is worse than his bite; although his words may be hurtful, his actions are benevolent.

**census** (n.)  an official count of populations, as one put forth by an authoritative agency; a survey or count that is systematically carried out

The government **census** illustrated how more and more families are choosing to move out of commercial areas and into more remote neighborhoods.

Officials at the **Census** for Forest Life have determined that the deer population at the nature preserve is too dense, threatening the longevity of the population living there.

According to a recent **census** study, more and more college graduates are moving back home as they enter the job market.

**documents** (v.) writes down, records, takes notes; makes a tangible record of something by filming or recording it; provides evidence by supplying substantiating information

> Using an online data management system, Dr. Dean thoroughly **documents** every one of his patient's visits.

> A talented film director, Kevin uses his camcorder to **document** landmark developments and achievements in his community.

> Every phone call received by the customer service department is thoroughly **documented** in the company's online client relations system and given a case reference number.

**ecosystem** (n.) a local, tightly woven group of interdependent organisms living within a particular environment; a bionetwork; an ecological unit; an environment complete with its flora and fauna

> At the Maritime Wharf Center, budding marine biologists, Harriet and Margaret, eagerly study seaside **ecosystems** alongside their marine mentor.

> Some consider a city to be a scar on the body of nature; others consider a metropolitan center to be a veritable, thriving **ecosystem** that exemplifies the balance of nature.

> Their biology professor took the class on several field trips each semester so that they could observe and study **ecosystems** such as forests, waterfalls, and marshes in their natural settings.

**encompasses** (v.) includes a broad, wide, or comprehensive range of ideas or elements; encircles, surrounds, or envelops

> At the precious age of six, Lucas **encompasses** all that his parents dream of for him: vitality, joy, and enthusiasm for life.

> The life of a mother **encompasses** myriad roles that include social director, stylist, manager, personal shopper, records keeper, chef, and chauffeur.

> His spacious home **encompasses** twelve rooms, three fireplaces, and four bathrooms.

**indistinguishable** (adj.)   impossible to tell apart; very hard to detect or understand; indistinct; vague; ambiguous

> The same make, model, and year, the two cars are **indistinguishable** at a glance; however, upon close inspection, one is deep midnight blue and the other is black.

> The voices of the twins, Lauren and Nina, are **indistinguishable** to Lena, who hears one as mellifluous and sprightly as the other.

> When they are seated on the couch in the family room, Yola has a hard time telling one of her close-in-age sons from the other; same haircut and attire, the young men at a glance appear **indistinguishable**.

**minuscule** (adj.)   very tiny; exceedingly small or insignificant; infinitesimal

> When one fathoms the misfortunes experienced throughout the globe, one's own problems seem minor and **minuscule**.

> Excessively focused on her outward appearance, the self-possessed actress had a **minuscule** birthmark removed that was the size of a pinhead!

> All of the **minuscule**, trivial, and tedious issues of the world add up to, what her mother used to call, "the daily minutiae."

**stance** (n.)   one's position or point of view on a topic or issue; an individual's way of standing; the bodily position of an athlete, such as a baseball player or golfer; one's attitude, outlook, or standpoint on a subject or person; one's posture, carriage, or positioning

> The younger brother strove to imitate his older brother's batting **stance**.

> "Be an upstanding human and take a firm **stance** against all forms of bullying and belittling," urged Ms. Salan, director of Anti-Bullying Allies.

> What is your **stance** on sustainability?

**submersibles** (n.)   objects that are designed or intended to be immersed under the water

> For his fifth birthday, Chester received an assortment of **submersibles** to play with in the pool, including torpedoes, diving sticks, and mini scuba divers.

> Packing for his vacation in Cabo San Lucas, the young man packed his goggles, swim flippers, scuba gear, and other **submersibles**.

> A robotlike **submersible** vessel was used to study the ocean bottom site of the "unsinkable" cruise liner, the *Titanic*.

**tendrilous** (adj.)   relating to the thin, threadlike parts of plants that attach and coil around an object, such as a fence, to give the plant support and stability; relating to a delicate coil or twist of green stem or human hair

> The green **tendrilous** growths of the tomato plants wrapped around the white lattice that was propped against the side of the backyard shed.

> Clematis is a beautiful flowering plant whose **tendrilous** vines can climb several feet high up the wall of a house.

> **Tendrilous** obstacles weave themselves into the characters' lives as they struggle to loosen their tight grip.

## MEMORY TIPS

Use these mnemonics (memory devices) to boost your vocabulary. Make up your own memory clues for words in this lesson that are personally challenging. Add these tips, and your own, to your Vocabulary Notebook.

### minuscule
**Minuscule** derives from the word *minus*, to make smaller. As a prefix, *min-* means "little" or "small." Think of its usage in *minute, minor, miniature, minicomputer*, and *miniskirt*. Granules of salt are **minuscule** in size compared to colored sprinkles.

### submersible
Link this word to *submarine*. Also note that the prefix *sub-* means "under" or "below." Think of *subway, subatomic*, and *subterranean* ("below the earth's surface"). **Submersibles** are vehicles, vessels, crafts, or other objects that can function under water without sustaining damage.

## MATCHING

Match the vocabulary words in Column A with their defining characteristics in Column B.

**Column A**

1. minuscule
2. ecosystem
3. stance
4. submersible
5. apparent

**Column B**

A. bionetwork of interdependent organisms

B. an underwater vessel or craft

C. very tiny

D. one's view or position on an issue

E. hard to discern differences between

F. clearly understood

G. pertaining to threadlike parts of plants that curl, wind, and twist

## WORDS IN CONTEXT

Based on the context in which each **bold** word is used, identify the word usage of each sentence as either C (Correct) or I (Incorrect).

1. It is **apparent** that narcissistic Nancy cares more about her own issues than those of others.

2. "The serving size of those steamed vegetable dumplings is **minuscule**," Andre thought to himself. "I could eat a dozen of those easily."

3. The oratory of the speech and debate competitor has a flimsy **stance**, for his speech is firmly focused and supported.

4. Elegantly floating, the candle **submersibles** illuminated the woods as they drifted across the lake.

5. Jackie's memoir **encompasses** the full gamut of her experience, as she disregards the lows and misfortunes and accentuates only the positive aspects of her life.

# Part V
# English Test Vocabulary

The English Test is primarily a test of grammar and usage. Punctuation, sentence structure, and proper use of standard idioms are tested as well. Nonetheless, I have seen in my practice how students' confusion about vocabulary causes them to answer English Test questions incorrectly. Edifying your vocabulary can substantially improve your performance on this section of the ACT test. Examples are taken from real and actual ACT tests.

## What types of questions will I encounter on the ACT English Test?

A wide variety of questions will be asked on this verbal test. Questions will pertain to your knowledge of the conventions of standard, written English. The questions break down into two main categories: Rhetorical Skills and Usage and Mechanics, as follows:

- Rhetorical Skills (style, organization, writing strategy, rhetorical and figurative devices)
- Usage and Mechanics (sentence structure, dependent and independent clauses, placement of modifying clauses and phrases, punctuation, grammar and usage)

Note that spelling is not tested on this exam.

Here are some of the more specific question types you are likely to encounter.

- How to use the following types of **punctuation** correctly: commas, apostrophes, dashes, semicolons, colons, periods, question marks, quotation marks, and exclamation points.
- How to correctly use **superlative** and **comparative** modifiers (*faster, fastest; wiser, wisest; better, best; more, most;* etc.).
- How to maintain consistent and active (not passive) **verb tense** and, depending on the sequence of events, use alternating verb tenses logically and soundly.
- How to use the correct case (objective or subjective) and form of **pronouns**; for example, *their/they're/there; its/it's; I/me; we/us.* Note: *its'* often appears in the ACT English Test, but *its'* is a decoy (or trap) answer because this word in fact does not exist in the English language.
- How to ensure that the writing is most effective in terms of **clarity** and **conciseness** (succinctness with regard to language expression).
- How to express **sound sentence structure**, avoiding run-ons (such as fused sentences and commas splices) and avoiding sentence fragments.
- How to maintain **parallel form** in the phrasing within the passages.
- How to use correct **prepositions** (such as *in, from, by, to, with, near, toward*) when joining parts of sentences together.
- How to correctly phrase standard English **idiomatic expressions**. For example, "Lia prefers apples *to* apricots" (correct); "Lia prefers apples *over* apricots" (incorrect).

   More examples: "Hank is regarded *as* an all-star ball player" (correct); "Hank is regarded *to be* an all-star ball player" (incorrect).

   "Liam's work performance is consistent *with* his employer's expectations" (correct); "Liam's work performance is consistent *to* his employer's expectations" (incorrect).
- How to maintain **grammatical agreement** among various parts of the sentences within the passages. For example: subjects and verbs must agree with each other; pronouns and their antecedents (references) must agree in gender and number.

# Lesson 21

## Test Takers' Anecdotes

On an English Test passage titled "Antarctic Adventure," polar adventurers ski while being pulled by parachutelike sails. Initially, the sails pull the women and their supplies hundreds of miles in unfailing winds. But then the winds stop. One of the multiple-choice questions referred to this sentence: *For the next five days, <u>accordingly</u>, there was almost no wind, and the pair sailed only 34 miles.* Alina considered these choices:

    A. NO CHANGE
    B. otherwise,
    C. consequently,
    D. however,

Alina incorrectly picked *consequently* because she associates this word with negative outcomes or *consequences*. This is understandable; the context supports negativity because the lack of wind adversely affects the skiers' travel. The answer, though, is **however** because **however** more effectively accentuates the contrast between traveling with steady winds and traveling with little to no wind.

On a different passage, **ambiguous** was the culprit for Andre; his misunderstanding of this word was the primary reason he answered a multiple-choice question incorrectly. He didn't understand that a detail in the passage (**fresco**, also an unknown word to him) was **ambiguous** and unnecessary because he lacked understanding of the word **ambiguous**.

On a real practice ACT, Jenna was stumped by the term **balk**, which appeared not only in the English Test passage but also, and repetitively, in the answer choices. The English Test question appears as follows:

*At a certain age, many Americans I know would balk, refuse, and hesitate at the idea of adding a year or two to what they regard as their actual age.*

    29. A. NO CHANGE
        B. balk and hesitate
        C. refuse and balk
        D. balk

The correct answer is "D. Balk" because the other choices are redundant. Without knowing the meaning of **balk**, many students would find this question difficult. That same English Test contained these words: **lax**, **affected**, **indifferent**, **harbored**, **hoaxes**, **skepticism**, **cordial**, **breadth**, **keen**, **solemn**, **pining**, and **missionaries**.

An English Test question asked about the following revision: "Which sentence, if added, would best describe the magnitude and expansiveness of the New York City subway system today?" Since the student thought that **magnitude** meant "importance" (instead of "large in degree, size, or scale"), he missed the correct answer.

---

> **beneficiary, coherence, competence, culinary, exultant**
> **inexplicably, omit, preceding, regiment, relevant**

---

**beneficiary** (n.)   an individual who is the recipient of some type of benefit or gain; someone entitled to money or property, as set forth by a will, a trust, or an insurance policy; a receiver

Hilde named her husband as primary **beneficiary** of her life insurance policy; she designated her children as contingent **beneficiaries**.

The **beneficiary** of a substantial charitable gift, Lucy expressed her gratitude profusely.

Her three sons are the **beneficiaries** of her life insurance, equal shares per stirpes.

**coherence** (n.)   holding together in a credible and logic whole; unity; consistency

To write with **coherence**, the author should include pertinent and interrelated examples.

The attorney's closing argument was marked by such **coherence** that his position seemed seamlessly tenable.

His train of thought is difficult to follow, as it is marked by digressions, ramblings, and a lack of **coherence**.

**competence** (n.)   skill or ability, particularly that which is acquired through training, apprenticeship, or experience; aptitude; proficiency; capability

> As a downhill skier, he exhibits **competence** on the intermediate as well as black diamond trails.

> Her linguistic **competence** is evidenced by her ability to speak conversational French, Italian, and Portuguese with a remarkable degree of ease and fluency.

> As an astute and talented information technologist, Julian epitomizes both versatility and **competence**.

**culinary** (adj.)   pertaining to cooking and food; gastronomy

> A **culinary** enthusiast, Henry creates dishes brimming with texture, flavor, and aroma.

> Eager to expand her cooking repertoire, Jamara took **culinary** classes in French, Italian, and Thai cuisine.

> To her **culinary** delight, she dined out with her boyfriend at a different top-rated restaurant every Saturday evening.

**exultant** (adj.)   joyful; very happy and pleased, particularly about something that someone has achieved for him or herself; jubilant, elated; triumphant

> At homecoming, the cheerleaders led out an **exultant** cheer when the Vikings scored their third touchdown, taking the lead!

> On his sixth birthday, Luke was **exultant** about taking home his new five-pound playful puppy.

> Setting her eyes on the tall pile of festively wrapped birthday gifts, Tamika released an **exultant** scream of joy and excitement!

**inexplicably** (adv.)   unable to be explained or expressed; unable to be justified; enigmatically; unaccountably; curiously

> **Inexplicably**, the two women felt as if they had known each other for years, although they only met a few months ago.

> A compassionate and **inexplicable** emotional bond endured between the cousins for over fifty-five years.

> Ian **inexplicably** walked over to his neighbor and offered to mow his lawn, free of charge!

**omit** (v.)   to leave someone or something out, either accidentally or intentionally; to delete, eliminate, expunge

> **Omit** the sarcasm from your concluding paragraph; it leaves a bitter taste in the reader's mouth.

> Careful not to **omit** any essentials from the care package, she checked her packing list several times.

> Lara is severely allergic to eggs, so she **omitted** this ingredient from her muffin recipe.

**preceding** (adj.)   occurring just before something else; existing or happening prior to something else; coming at the beginning or before; former; earlier; previous

> **Preceding** their retirement, they traveled to seven different countries and took both eastern and western Caribbean cruises.

> "Eliminate the faulty comparison and improper diction from the **preceding** sentence," Sam's English teacher pleaded.

> On Backwards Day, the campers are thrilled to hear that their desserts will be served **preceding** their meals!

**regiment** (n.)   a unit of soldiers or officials; a large group of people or things that is orderly in conduct or organization; a brigade, division, or troop

> The rigorous workouts of the military **regiment** include sprinting, weight lifting, and high intensity interval training.

> The diligent **regiment** of upstanding young men and women was praised lavishly by the lieutenant.

> The troops of the Eastern Hills **Regiment** were ordered by the colonel to organize themselves into specialized military task units.

**relevant** (adj.)   characterized as being logically connected with something else; being significant to real world issues and affairs; germane, pertinent, applicable

> The issue of homelessness is **relevant** to a discussion about educational and workplace inequality.

> Active readers strive to absorb and visualize **relevant** details and references.

---

## MEMORY TIPS

Use these mnemonics (memory devices) to boost your vocabulary. Make up your own memory clues for words in this lesson that are personally challenging. Add these tips, and your own, to your Vocabulary Notebook.

### <u>pre</u>ceding
Let the prefix *pre-* (which means "first," "before," or "early") remind you that **preceding** refers to that which comes first or before. Notice that *pre-* is used in the following words: *premature, preamble, prequalify.*

### <u>rel</u>evant
Link *related* to **relevant**. Both words have three syllables, and start with the same three letters. Challenge yourself to learn these upper level synonyms for relevant: *germane* and *pertinent.*

## MATCHING

Match the vocabulary words in Column A with their defining characteristics in Column B.

**Column A**

1. inexplicably
2. omit
3. beneficiary
4. relevance
5. preceding

**Column B**

A. coming before; prior; before mentioned

B. pertaining to a particular matter or topic; significance

C. one entitled to money by will, and inheritance, or a trust

D. puzzling, in that something or some circumstance defies explanation

E. an army unit or military troop

F. triumphant and filled with joy

G. to leave out, to exclude

## WORDS IN CONTEXT

Based on the context in which each **bold** word is used, identify the word usage of each sentence as either C (Correct) or I (Incorrect).

1. A festive poolside cocktail party **preceded** the graduation ceremony.

2. Among her finest **attributes** are diligence, compassion, and resourcefulness.

3. Lisa's Instagram postings exhibit her **competence** as a photographer.

4. The restaurants off campus provide a **culinary** variety that includes Thai, Japanese, and Mexican foods.

5. Walter's **provocative** essay titles and lead sentences readily lose his readers' interest and attention.

# Lesson 22

## Test Takers' Anecdotes

On a Humanities passage about philosophy, Amanda answered the last question wrong because she had the wrong association for the word **fleeting**. In addition, she had a hard time deciphering the meaning of the lines referenced in the question: "With such **rudimentary** tools, you can perform ... **concrete** mark, bringing the **ethereal** interior into the public external world, **refining** it..." She said the sentence gave her a headache.

Connor is a science buff with an A in AP biology. He knew that the multiple-choice reading question was asking for the closest opposite to *expand*, (which he astutely located earlier in context). Yet, Connor did not know that the verb, **contract**, was the *best* opposite from among the four choices: *contract, reduce, decrease, compress*. Also, the precise meaning of **compress** ("reduce, as in making smaller or more compact") was a little fuzzy for him. Erroneously, he chose *reduce*.

Andre also found a question very tricky and answered it incorrectly because he didn't know what it meant for Joan, a character in the passage, to be **engrossed** ("absorbed, immersed, actively engaged") in her work. Ironically, Andre (perhaps because he was subliminally picking up on the middle part of the word, *gross*) thought the word had a negative connotation, such as "put off by" or "turned off by."

In an English passage titled "Diego Rivera: The People's Painter," the use of the word **wield** created some confusion for Tom. It was used several times in this context: "wield more political power." Tom wasn't sure if the verb **wield** meant to build power, to yield power, to exert power, or to enforce power. Because of his lack of clarity about this word's precise meaning, Tom felt ill-equipped to answer this question with confidence and accuracy. Consequently, he found himself guessing.

---

acute, alpha, civic, cunning, employed
exquisite, intrigued, kinship, unsuspecting, vitality

---

**acute** (adj.)   sharp, intense, keen in terms of intellect, ability, or perception; perceptively wise; having angles less than ninety degrees

> The abdominal pain was so **acute** that Connie held her breath and curled her toes.

> Jessica's sense of hearing is **acute**; she can hear conversations verbatim from one floor of the house to the next.

> As a Doctor of Optometry, Jaclyn strives to optimize her patients' visual health and **acuity**.

**alpha** (adj.)   pertaining to the one that is first, dominant, or most assertive in the dominance hierarchy of the animal world; the one who is most powerful or domineering in a group; relating to alphabetical order; (n.)   the first letter of the Greek alphabet

> Even though the miniature poodle, Tino, weighs eight pounds and Baci, the Labradoodle, weighs forty-five, Tino is the **alpha** dog who dominates the pair of well-loved pets.

> Despite Judd's being the accomplished breadwinner, Tina is the **alpha** female who dominates the household, the social calendar, and the decision making.

> The sophomore sorority pledges had to learn Alpha Fi's official oath, its songs, and the spoken and written Greek alphabet, which starts with **alpha** and ends with omega.

**civic** (adj.)   relating to the governments of cities, municipalities, and towns; pertaining to communities

> The **civic** association meeting addresses local concerns of interest to its members.

> **Civic** minded Cliff attends every community fund-raiser, parade, and ribbon cutting ceremony.

> Feeling a great deal of **civic** pride and community spirit, Sal delivers an exuberant speech at every **civic** reception.

**cunning** (adj.)   deceptive, guileful; misleading; manipulative; pertaining to an individual who should be regarded with suspicion and distrust

> Kurt's **cunning** and manipulative ways will soon get the better of him.

> **Cunning** Connor planned his next dupe on those he loosely referred to as his friends.

> At the end of their unplanned encounters, the sly and **cunning** coyote outwitted the naive rabbit each and every time!

**employed** (v.)   used something to accomplish a goal or task; utilized; involved in paid work or some activity; occupied; busy; engaged

> To carry numerous pieces of luggage to the second floor of the ski lodge, the Cunninghams **employed** the help of their brawny sons.

> The college student routinely **employed** a cell phone to provide himself with a personal WiFi hotspot when he found himself in an area without Internet service.

> The handy homeowner **employed** a hefty bobcat to excavate a space to build his backyard stone patio.

**exquisite** (adj.)   incredibly beautiful; gorgeous; intricate or delicate in workmanship; superbly fine

> On the **exquisite** necklace shone semiprecious crystals in an array of pastel colors.

> Raphaela's **exquisite** jewelry creations are individually designed and handcrafted.

> A setting of **exquisite** natural beauty, the lush and rolling mountain range surrounded the 900-acre university campus.

**intrigued** (v.)   schemed and used underhanded measures to accomplish a goal; plotted; connived; (adj.)   so intensely interested in something that one seeks to learn more

> The submarine building company **intrigued** to keep its industrial methods and technological processes undercover from potential competitors.

> Tirelessly, Tim met discreetly with attorneys and accountants, as he **intrigued** to gain control of Melissa's property and finances.

> **Intrigued** by the nature preserve's natural beauty, the friends hiked its many trails, photographed its wildlife, and studied its creeks and ponds.

**kinship** (n.)   close connection by marriage, family lineage, or adoption; relationship felt as a strong bond between people who may or may not be related by blood; a general relatedness between things, nations, fields of study, people, communities

> As Romance languages, Italian, Portuguese, and Spanish share a linguistic **kinship**.

> Though he was born in the heart of Providence, Rhode Island, Chuck claims **kinship** with the Southeastern states.

> Feeling a strong sense of familial **kinship**, Diana and Eva are more like sisters than college friends.

**unsuspecting** (adj.)   without suspicions pertaining to someone, somebody, or some situation; unaware, unwitting; unwary

> **Unsuspecting** sidewalk shoppers are most likely to be victims of pickpocketing.

> Naïve Nellie and Trusting Tim divulged their personal plans to their neighbor, **unsuspecting** his having ulterior motives.

> **Unsuspecting** of the impending storm, the Kubler family left home for a long hike along the country roads.

**vitality** (n.)   an individual's abundant life force or drive; great mental and/or physical energy usually combined with happiness and vigor; energy, liveliness; verve

> To increase his **vitality** and mental acuity, Hugh drinks a vegetable-and-fruit-packed "Green Machine" smoothie every morning.

> A night owl, Gwendolyn feels a surge of **vitality** between ten o'clock at night and two in the morning!

> Nicknamed "Slug," Sam surprised his new friends with his energetic spirit and sustained bursts of **vitality**!

## MEMORY TIPS

Use these mnemonics (memory devices) to boost your vocabulary. Make up your own memory clues for words in this lesson that are personally challenging. Add these tips, and your own, to your Vocabulary Notebook.

**acute**
In mathematics, consider how acute angles (less than 90 degrees), relative to obtuse angles (more than 90 degrees), form more pointed angles and, therefore, have *sharper* points. Link this geometry definition to the definition of **acute** as "*sharp*-minded, keen, perceptive."

**alpha**
In the Greek alphabet, **alpha** is the first letter. Accordingly, let **alpha** remind you of "first," "beginning," "leading," and "highest in rank."

**vitality**
In Latin, *vita* means "life." *Vi-* and *viva-* are also prefixes and word stems that indicate "life." Consider these root words' use in words and phrases such as: *vi*tamin, *vi*tal, *vi*gor, *viva*cious, con*vi*vial, and curriculum *vi*tae.

## MATCHING

Match the vocabulary words in Column A with their defining characteristics in Column B.

| Column A | Column B |
| --- | --- |
| 1. civic | A. a strong life force, drive, or energy level |
| 2. vitality | B. strikingly beautiful |
| 3. kinship | C. pertaining to cities, towns, governments |
| 4. implement | D. keenly interested in something or someone |
| 5. exquisite | E. to put into effect |
| | F. a strong sense of connection or relation |
| | G. unaware, lacking a sense of suspicion |

## WORDS IN CONTEXT

Based on the context in which each **bold** word is used, identify the word usage of each sentence as either C (Correct) or I (Incorrect).

1. Although Connor and Casey are not blood relatives, they felt the **kinship** of cousins.

2. **Unsuspecting** and inexperienced tourists traveled to hurricane-prone islands during the peak of tropical storm season.

3. Of the two pets, one a large breed and the other a toy breed, the eight-pound poodle boldly asserted himself as **alpha** dog!

4. To secure the skis and poles on the rooftop ski rack, Emil **employed** a set of bungee cords and Velcro straps.

5. **Intrigued** by looming bracelets out of small rubber bands, the first grader made colorful bracelets for himself as well as for friends and relatives!

# Lesson 23

## Test Takers' Anecdotes

Brad missed a placement question because he didn't know what a **clearing** was. (Placement questions ask the student to determine the most effective placement of a sentence to maintain logic and coherence within a paragraph.) He thought that "there" in sentence 3 could only follow "trail," which appeared in sentence 1, because he did not know that a **clearing** is also a place. Brian said he had no idea and had never heard of this word.

The word **preceding** presents confusion for many students and appears several times within the English Test questions. Timmy, for example, thought "**preceding** paragraph" meant the following paragraph, so he was ill-equipped to answer a question about transitions and got it wrong. Maybe students associate **preceding** with *proceeding*?

George was confused by an answer choice in which the word **scarcely** appeared: "By the turn of the century, there was **scarcely** a wolf left in the state." He thought **scarcely** had to do with *scary* and so, as a result, George did not pick this answer choice, which turned out to be correct. This breakdown in meaning, caused primarily by the misunderstanding of one word, cost this test taker this English Test question.

---

**agronomist, immersion, imperial, recounted, redeeming
rivals, scarcely, stifle, subsequently, unsolicited**

---

**agronomist** (n.)   a person who studies the scientific and technological aspects of using plants for food and fuel; one who deals with interactions among plants, soils, and the environment

> **Agronomist** Igor investigates how soil management relates to crop production.

> As an **agronomist**, Peter experiments with crop rotation, drainage, plant breeding, and weed control.

> Beyond these lines of inquiry, an **agronomist** examines the interplay between soil conditions and pest control.

**immersion** (n.)   complete absorption or involvement; relating to something that occupies one's time, concentration, and energy; deeply engaged in an activity, some study, a language, a culture, or an endeavor

> A firm believer in complete cultural **immersion**, Richard landed in Turkey without knowing a soul and without a room to rent.

> Foreign language **immersion** can be an effective way for students to learn and excel in mastering a foreign tongue, since typically teachers use the foreign language almost exclusively throughout lessons.

> **Immersed** in soul-searching, Miranda meditated daily, practiced yoga several times a week, and often read spiritually themed books.

**imperial** (adj.)   relating to an empire or emperor; pertaining to one country's authority over another; holding supreme power; majestic

> The **imperial** palace is a lavish display of crystal chandeliers, antique furnishings, and fine collectibles.

> Exhibiting grace, charity, and social composure, the **imperial** family is a role model for citizens.

> Justina named her cosmetics company, **Imperial** Beauty, in order to conjure up images of royalty, aristocracy, and princess status among her affluent patrons.

**recounted** (v.)   told a tale about something or someone; described, delineated, or narrated the details of a story; reported

> In vivid detail, the vivacious six-year-old **recounted** to us his thrilling ride on the Tower of Terror at Splish Splash Water Park.

> The film documentarian has **recounted**, through his multimedia films, the rise of numerous grassroots volunteer organizations that cater to the immediate and real needs of the community.

> **Recount** for us how he romantically proposed to you at Freeport Beach during sunset.

**redeeming** (adj.)   compensating for flaws or shortcomings; serving to make up for a defect; favorable

> **Redeeming** features of the college's rundown residential hall are its spacious common area and quiet study lounges.

> The strong-willed toddler's **redeeming** feature was his adorable looks.

> His soft gaze and warm hug are powerful and **redeeming** forces that always draw her back into his strong arms.

**rivals** (n.)   adversaries, foes, competitors; (v.) contends; competes; vies

> Are you **rivals** in the classroom, or just foes on the soccer field?

> In light of the patient's well-being and comfort, the relatives disagree heatedly and have unfortunately become **rivals** instead of allies.

> The ten-year-old Labrador Retriever's energy and playful antics **rival** those of a rambunctious new puppy.

**scarcely** (adj.)   only to the slightest degree; almost certainly not; surely not; not quite; only just; hardly, merely, barely

> The hired party helper **scarcely** lifted a finger to assist the frustrated hosts at the out-of-control pool party.

> Henry **scarcely** took a bite of the sautéed jumbo shrimp when he affirmatively announced, "I do not eat seafood."

> Given the spending cutbacks, there are **scarcely** enough resources to indulge the desires of each member of the community.

**stifle** (v.)   to suppress, crush, or end, often by force; to block the development of something; to suffocate; to stop a yawn, sneeze, or cough before it starts

> Nicknamed Sabrina the Sabotage, the envious woman **stifled** her cousin's spirited entrepreneurial endeavors.

> A soulful, caring, and mutually edifying love connection should never be severed or **stifled**.

> "Do not **stifle** a society's or an individual's cherished customs and beliefs!" exclaimed the passionate sociology professor.

**subsequently** (adj.)   after, later, following; next; consequently

> Lila lost ten pounds on the South Beach eating plan; **subsequently**, she maintained a healthy weight by primarily consuming lean meats, fish, whole grains, and vegetables.

> The employee's **subsequently** discovered misconduct should not impede her from advancing at the boutique law firm.

> **Subsequent** to her employment at the design company, Jacinta became artistic director of a prestigious Manhattan-based sports marketing firm.

**unsolicited** (adj.)   received without being requested; unasked for; unwarranted

> Nosy Nellie offers **unsolicited** advice to those who she determines would benefit from her pearls of wisdom.

> Most **unsolicited** book manuscripts end up in the managing editor's slush pile.

> Spam clutters her email in-box to such an extent that she religiously unsubscribes to each and every **unsolicited** message she receives.

---

## MEMORY TIPS

Use these mnemonics (memory devices) to boost your vocabulary. Make up your own memory clues for words in this lesson that are personally challenging. Add these tips, and your own, to your Vocabulary Notebook.

### agronomist
*Agro-* is derived from the French and Greek and means "pertaining to fields and soil." Think of its use in words and phrases such as agriculture, agrarian, and agro-industrial.

### recounted
Did you know that a *raconteur* is a storyteller? Let *raconteur* cue you into the meaning of the action verb, **recount** ("to tell a story, to narrate"). For auditory and visual learners, this mnemonic device can be effective, as *raconteur* and **recount** look and sound similar.

## MATCHING

Match the vocabulary words in Column A with their defining characteristics in Column B.

**Column A**

1. unsolicited
2. immersion
3. recounted
4. agronomist
5. rivals

**Column B**

A. adversaries, competitors; contenders

B. one who studies farming procedures

C. narrated a story; told

D. favorable, positive

E. a style or type of teaching

F. relating to kings, queens, royals

G. not asked for, not sought out

## WORDS IN CONTEXT

Based on the context in which each **bold** word is used, identify the word usage of each sentence as either C (Correct) or I (Incorrect).

1. Buddies off the ball field, they **rival** heatedly on the diamond during playoffs.

2. The **agronomist** carefully decided on the best course of treatment for his patient who suffered from both glaucoma and high blood pressure.

3. Kurt's contentious nature is one of his most **redeeming** qualities.

4. Buck's intense, irascible personality **stifles** Margaret's lightheartedness and positivity.

5. All mandates are honored at the **Imperial** Court, which is presided over by royals and dignitaries.

# Lesson 24

## Test Takers' Anecdotes

Brad missed a question because he didn't know the meaning of **kinship**. The question asked about a **relevant** detail that "suggests the unity of the people." Not only did Brad not know the meaning of **kinship**, but he also defined **relevant** as "logical," an imprecise definition that can be misleading when choosing his answer.

On an English passage about Roberto Clemente, Hailey incorrectly answered a diction, or word choice, question. Hailey selected **entitled**, making the sentence read, "He (Clemente) was **entitled** the National League Batting Champion four times..." The correct answer was "named." Sometimes the correct answers are basic words, but the words among the choices can be distracting when they are fuzzy or unknown.

On an English passage titled "Three Stars, Many Stories," Maggie encountered an obstacle in the following question because she did not know the meaning of **allusion**: "Given that all the choices are true, which one ends this paragraph with the clearest **allusion** to Orion, as the constellation is described later in the essay?"

---

> **adorned, angler, coalition, compelling, emphatic
> exemplifies, fixed, humanitarian, implemented, orient**

---

**adorned** (adj.)   decorated; enhanced with ornaments and decorative accessories; bedecked; made more ornate; embellished

Black iron scrolls handcrafted by their great-grandfather, Vittorio, **adorned** the walls that flanked the family room's fieldstone fireplace.

Harriet's long blonde hair was **adorned** with floral hair clips from J. Crew.

The Simonson's front porch is **adorned** with lion statuary and large terra-cotta planters.

**angler** (n.)   a fisher; a person who fishes for sport

At the annual Snapper Derby, the **anglers** fished for blues and flounder as well as snappers.

The Captree party fishing boat was filled with **anglers** who loved the smell of saltwater, the sounds of the sea and seagulls, and the taste of freshly grilled fish drizzled with lemon.

Asking each other, "Any nibbles?" the enthusiastic **anglers** lined the Sea Cliff Beach boardwalk, eager to catch their evening meals.

**coalition** (n.)   an alliance; a union into one body or group with similar interests or a guiding purpose

The grassroots **Coalition** to Eradicate Local Hunger met every other Friday to plan their next food drive or fund-raiser.

A literacy **coalition** was established to emphasize reading and vocabulary across all academic disciplines.

Pushing their acrimonious past aside, Butch and Theo decided to become allies in the fight against crime and formed a neighborhood watch **coalition**.

**compelling** (adj.)   attracting, commanding, and maintaining a great deal of attention; engrossing; alluring; forcing an individual to behave in a certain manner; strongly convincing

A **compelling** speaker, Victoria kept her audience glued to her every word.

Her business ideas are **compelling**, and the queries from her wide-eyed peers are continual.

Inwardly, Lidia felt **compelled** to go down to the boardwalk to watch the fireworks with her family, for her late father's birthday is the Fourth of July.

**emphatic** (adj.)   definite; certain; stated or executed with emphasis; insistent

"May I stay out until three in the morning?" asked Gus. "Absolutely not!" Mom answered, **emphatically**.

Julian's rejection of Julia's idea was **emphatic**; he would not budge on his firmly-rooted decision.

When it comes to her diet, she is **emphatic**. She refuses to eat processed foods, fatty meats, and sugary desserts.

**exemplifies** (v.)   serves as a prime example or model; illustrates in a manner that makes something more clearly understood

Actively practicing daily acts of kindness, kindhearted Kendra **exemplifies** charity and compassion.

The team loyalty demonstrated by the Vikings baseball team **exemplifies** dedication, camaraderie, and commitment.

Can you **exemplify** your statement with several specific scenarios?

**fixed** (adj.)   not subject to change in form, amount, or time; securely held into current position; unchanging; permanent; static; unwavering

Evidently in love, Leo kept his soulful eyes adoringly **fixed** on Catarina.

The couple slowly but steadily learned how difficult it is to support the increasing needs of a maturing family on a **fixed** income.

Now a college sophomore, Alicia has committed to the seven-year joint degree program and her course of study seems **fixed** and steady.

**humanitarian** (adj.)   dedicated to improving the welfare and happiness of individual people and communities; caring and compassionate toward others; (n) an individual who is devoted to humanitarian efforts

> The boys' **humanitarian** efforts included a food drive, a beach cleanup, and gift deliveries to needy families during the holiday season.

> **Humanitarian** personalities are those that think outside of themselves, seeking to promote the well-being of others less fortunate.

> A devoted **humanitarian**, Hugh participates in several charity walks, fund-raisers, and philanthropic events each season.

**implemented** (v.)   put into effect or action; carried out a plan or sequence of events; executed

> Hattie **implemented** a spring-cleaning plan for her home that included purging unneeded items, dusting every surface and corner, and burning candles in soothing natural fragrances.

> Once their plan of action was **implemented**, the Coopers carried out their tasks diligently and enthusiastically.

> A sound financial business plan has yet to be **implemented** by the co-directors of the newbie company.

**orient** (v.)   to adjust with relation to surroundings or circumstances; to familiarize an individual with new surroundings or circumstances; to place in a particular position in relation to something else; to determine the position of; to get one's bearings

> To **orient** her sons toward the game of golf, she signed them up for summer golf clinics and took them to the driving range.

> The summer program is designed to **orient** the incoming freshmen to the university, its programs, its facilities, and its surroundings.

> The couple **oriented** the metal wall hanging of a sun so that it faced the pool and lounge chairs.

## MEMORY TIPS

Use these mnemonics (memory devices) to boost your vocabulary. Make up your own memory clues for words in this lesson that are personally challenging. Add these tips, and your own, to your Vocabulary Notebook.

### coalition

The popular prefix, co-, means "with" or "together." Consider the use of co- in words such as community, copilot, cohabitate, committee, and coalesce. Connect this prefix meaning to the meaning of the **coalition**: a group working "together," or allied with each other.

### exemplifies

Allow the sound and sight of this word to remind you of the word *example*. If Mother **exemplifies** patience, then her manner and conduct serve as a leading *example* of patience. The Statue of Liberty **exemplifies** freedom.

### orient

Think of the **Orient** as a geographical location on the map. Link this understanding to the meaning of **orient** that has to do with positioning one thing in relation to other things. Think of college *orient*ation as a time during which freshman **orient** themselves to the new surroundings of their campus, dormitories, and facilities.

## MATCHING

Match the vocabulary words in Column A with their defining characteristics in Column B.

**Column A**

1. coalition
2. angler
3. compelling
4. fixed
5. humanitarian

**Column B**

A. a fisherman; surfcaster

B. a group of allies united for a common goal

C. showing concern for mankind; benevolent

D. to position something toward a certain direction or toward a certain subject

E. engrossing or alluring

F. serves as a model example of something

G. unmoving, status quo

## WORDS IN CONTEXT

Based on the context in which each **bold** word is used, identify the word usage of each sentence as either C (Correct) or I (Incorrect).

1. To **orient** himself in the woods, the hiker took out his compass.

2. The **fixed** rate of return on his investment fluctuates between five and ten percent.

3. Competitive and fractious are the words that come to mind when one hears the term **coalition**.

4. The experienced golf caddie **exemplifies** diligence, knowledge of the course, and prime physical condition.

5. As the college campus lacked a club soccer team, a group of sophomores **implemented** an intercollegiate fall league.

# Lesson 25

## Test Takers' Anecdotes

Bruce had trouble with this question on the English Test:

> *Producing the film long before interplanetary explorations
> had begun, Melies could* <u>arouse</u> *his audience's curiosity with
> unconstrained fantasy.*

Which of the following alternatives to the underlined word would
be LEAST acceptable?

A. whet
B. stimulate
C. awaken
D. disturb

Brian said he felt confused by the word **whet**, and said that he had never
seen it before. He ended up picking this word, thinking that the ACT would
want the hard word as the answer. It turned out, though, that the unac-
ceptable choice was "disturb." Had Brian known the meaning of **whet**,
he would have understood that this action verb worked effectively in the
context of the passage.

Tara missed a question about transitional language because, as she
expressed it, she had no idea what **nevertheless** (which appeared in the
English passage) meant, although she admitted to having encountered
this curious word several times before.

The meaning of **kinship** caused some lack of understanding for Pete,
preventing him from answering an English Test question correctly.

> **assertion, bravado, chide, detracts, honed**
> **odyssey, sojourner, staggering, undaunted, whet**

**assertion** (n.)   a statement of opinion or belief; an emphatic statement that one believes to be true; a declaration; an affirmation

> Based on your dreamy **assertions** and visions of grandeur, it is evident that your mind is not grounded in the hard facts of reality.

> "Is your statement a fact-based **assertion**, or merely your opinion?" Abed inquired.

> Just because one makes an **assertion**, the statement isn't necessarily taken as fact.

**bravado** (n.)   a showy display of boldness; boasting, audacity; an affected or authentic display of self-confidence and courage

> Timorous, tongue-tied Timmy practiced his conversational **bravado** daily in front of a full-length mirror.

> Sometimes the most insecure people are the more likely to speak with **bravado**.

> Despite his incessant **bravado**, Kurt was a weak man in both mind and spirit.

**chide** (v.)   to gently reprimand, scold, or reproach; to tell someone off; to vocally disapprove of someone's actions; to express that you are displeased with someone's behavior

> Do not **chide** me for trying. Those who don't try are those who fear failure.

> Regardless of his parents' **chiding**, the wayward teen continued to dig himself into deeper trouble.

> Chuck **chided** his dogs for barking at even the slightest of household noises.

**detracts** (v.) lessens, makes smaller or less valuable; reduces the importance or quality of something

> A stern, self-assured facial expression **detracts** from her kind words.

> Misaligned teeth **detract** from a genuine, warm smile.

> Today's soupy humidity **detracts** from an otherwise, warm sunny afternoon.

**hone** (v.) to sharpen or improve something with practice and refinements; to polish over time, as in one's skills; to sharpen a blade on a whetstone

> Daily practice **hones** Justin's accomplished violin playing skills.

> Justina's baking abilities were gradually **honed** over two decades of recipe following, tweaking, and taste testing.

> Dressed head to toe in neon orange, the long-bearded hunter deftly **hones** his blade on the edge of the boulder.

**odyssey** (n.) a long, epic journey; an expedition; an extended trip during which many notable events occur

> *The Odyssey* by Homer, a classic work of fiction, chronicles the long journey of Kind Odysseus as his wife awaits his homecoming.

> Meditation, prayer, and conscious kindness are all part of Liv's personal **odyssey** of self-discovery.

> With a ride to the airport, a connecting flight, an airport delay, and a cab ride in traffic, the five-hour journey seemed more like an **odyssey** than a business commute.

**sojourner** (n.)  a vacationer; one who travels and stays in a place for a temporary period of time

> A spirited **sojourner** aboard a catamaran, Richard writes a riveting travel blog to keep his friends and family back home informed.

> Casual **sojourners**, the family enjoyed weekend trips during the summer and early fall to Martha's Vineyard, Rhode Island, and Block Island.

> During her **sojourn** in Paris, she picked up on the subtleties of French cuisine, decorating aesthetic, and vanguard fashion style.

**staggering** (adj.)  tending to overwhelm or astonish; fascinating; astounding; astonishing

> A **staggering** number of mosquitoes flocked around the campsite, as each and every camper sprayed bug repellant head to toe.

> The attorney's six-figure fees were **staggering**.

> Walking across the Grand Canyon on a tightrope cable, aerialist Nik Wallenda accomplished the **staggering** feat of courage, determination, and mental strength.

**undaunted** (adj.)  characterized as not being held back by the prospects of loss, failure, or defeat; unafraid, brave, resolute, fearless; intrepid

> **Undaunted** by a series of unfortunate developments, Luke persevered with faith and strength.

> The throng of preteens, **undaunted** and visibly excited, entered the haunted mansion.

> Facing many unknowns, Liliana steadfastly remains hopeful, centered, and **undaunted**.

**whet** (v.)   to sharpen, as in a feeling, skill, or interest; to stimulate or awaken; to sharpen a weapon or blade by rubbing it on a stone

> The televised get-rich-quick scheme **whetted** Tim's appetite for making money fast!

> "Before carving that turkey, **whet** your knife on this stone," Cary advised.

> Does listening to theatrical show tunes **whet** your interest in attending Broadway's next critically acclaimed play?

---

## MEMORY TIPS

Use these mnemonics (memory devices) to boost your vocabulary. Make up your own memory clues for words in this lesson that are personally challenging. Add these tips, and your own, to your Vocabulary Notebook.

### sojourner
Notice the word *journey* within **so*jour*ner**? This visual mnemonic clue can help you remember that a **sojourner** is one who travels or takes a *journey*.

### staggering
A stag is a male deer. Some adult stags can weigh close to three hundred pounds. Now that is a **staggering** weight! Recall that **staggering** means tending to astonish or fascinate. Here's an alliterative picture clue: Stately and strapping, the staggering stag strolled stoically.

### undaunted
Think of *unhaunted* (a made-up word) as a way of remembering the meaning of this word. **Undaunted** (*unhaunted*), Leo entered the undulating doorway of the haunted house.

## MATCHING

Match the vocabulary words in Column A with their defining characteristics in Column B.

| Column A | Column B |
|---|---|
| 1. whet | A. to arouse an interest, spark an idea |
| 2. chide | B. fascinating, astonishing |
| 3. assertion | C. carefree, unworried; not frazzled; stoic |
| 4. detracts | D. a declaration, a strong statement |
| 5. undaunted | E. lessens, diminishes; takes away from |
| | F. to reprimand, blame, or scold |
| | G. a display of audacity |

## WORDS IN CONTEXT

Based on the context in which each **bold** word is used, identify the word usage of each sentence as either C (Correct) or I (Incorrect).

1. Over the course of a few years, Lisa's photography skills became so refined and **honed** that her pictures looked flawless and professional.

2. He packed light for his extended weekend **sojourn**, carrying only a small duffle bag and a compact backpack.

3. The **odyssey** to the scenic Whaling Marina was ten minutes by car.

4. Not even a fleeting worry could **detract** from the meditative atmosphere of the drum circle held at Sunset Park.

5. To **whet** her children's interest in sailing, Andrea signed them up for a series of summer regattas.

# Part VI
# Writing Test Vocabulary

The Writing Test is otherwise known as the essay portion of the ACT. More often than not, the ACT writing topics pertain to the life of a high school student or issues that students would most likely find of interest or concern. A survey of real ACT essay prompts from the current online test, and a few former tests, reveals that the following topics are the most prevalent:

- Should a certain number of **community service** hours be required for graduation?
- Should high schools have **separate** classrooms for **males and females**?
- Should a **dress code** be part of high school policy?
- Should the **length** of high school be extended to five years instead of four?
- Should students be required to log a certain number of **volunteer** or paid **work** hours in order to receive a diploma?
- Should a certain percentage of **television** programming be devoted to **educational** topics?
- Should teachers and students share equally in being **responsible for students' education**, or does this responsibility rest more with one group than the other.

# Lesson 26

This lesson offers alternatives for words students tend to overuse when writing. The purpose of this lesson is to help students enhance their vocabulary variety in the ACT essay. Synonyms, phrases, and variations are provided for words that are likely to be used with high frequency, given the nature of typical essay prompts:

**activities**, leisure pursuits, pastimes, hobbies, clubs, after-school commitments

**classes**, courses, APs, Regents classes, Honors classes, electives, coursework, internships, independent study, math or science research

**classroom**, library, homeroom, office, lecture hall, conference room

**coaches**, mentors, trainers, facilitators, counselors, tutors, motivators, team leaders

**community service**, volunteer work, volunteerism, community outreach, local support efforts

**debate**, mock trial, speech and debate, argument, student jury, peer court

**dress code**, attire, outfits, apparel, clothing, uniforms, dress conformity

**education**, schooling, training, enrichment, scholarly achievement, secondary school education, undergraduate education.

**experience**, involvement, participation, background, memberships

**extracurricular activities**, clubs, organizations, memberships, offices held

**grades**, marks, GPA, cumulative average, transcript, academic ratings, evaluation

**homework**, learning, enrichment, assignments, at-home projects, studying

**policy**, requirements, responsibilities, procedures, code of conduct, academic integrity code

**school**, high school, college prep, boarding school, private school, secondary school, specific name of high school

**students**, peers, classmates, learners, college-bound

**success**, achievement, ranking, accomplishments, attainment, honors, awards, distinctions, medals

**teachers**, educators, instructors, faculty, staff, mentors, advisors, advocates

**technology**, computer literacy, skill, expertise, technology know-how

Outlined here are a few small, but tricky words you should add to your review. They often confuse test-takers, and as such they are tested on the ACT English Test. Study them for the English Test, but also know how to use them correctly in your essay.

**it's / its / its'**
**it's ("it is")**

It's a picture perfect beach day!

Why bother locking the safe; it's empty.

**its (singular possessive pronoun)**

Round and round in circles, the kitten chases its tail.

The freshly baked bread is just coming out of the oven. Its aroma is wafting throughout the house.

**its'**

This is a tricky imposter found on the ACT; this word does not actually exist!

**there / their / they're**

**there (pronoun indicating a place)**

Paris sounds like a dream city I wish to visit there one day in the near future.

"Tim, where do you live?" asked Gus. "I live way up there," answered Tim, pointing to the log cabin at the top of the mountain.

**their (plural possessive pronoun)**

Everyone in the Guinness family is a diehard football fan. A game is not a game without their presence in the bleachers.

Their parents never miss a football game, whether it is home or away.

**they're (they are)**

Buy your ski jackets and pants in the spring because they're on sale then.

Buy two outfits. They're on a two-for-one sale this week!

**too / two / to**
**too (means "very")**

It is too hot to do more than sit around and sip lemonade in the shade.

It is too cold to make the thirty-minute trek across campus to the gym.

**two (the number "2")**

His favorite McDonald's meal is menu item number two.

I would like to order two medium fries, please.

**to (a preposition used to connect parts of a sentence)**

The fastest way to get to Jones Beach is to take the Meadowbrook Parkway.

To turn a corner, create a new and positive habit in your life.

**than / then**
**than (used in comparisons)**

Gucci bags are more fashionable than those carried at the new Madison Avenue boutique.

I like grilled fish better than baked.

**then (means "next," "in addition," "in that case")**

First we went to the beach; then we stopped at the mall.

Go ten miles west, then head north onto rural Route 17.

**who / whom**
**who (subjective pronoun case)**

Who are you asking to the senior prom?

Who is banging at the front door?

**whom (objective pronoun case)**

To whom would you give the most credit for the success of the fund-raiser?

This amazing screenplay was written by whom?

**who's / whose**
**who's (who is)**

Who's at the door?

Tell us who's starring in the upcoming movie.

**whose (possessive case)**

Whose gloves are these?

Within whose heart does yours rest?

# Memory Tips Reviewed

For easy reference, this section restates all of the memory tips provided in the individual lessons contained within this book. Once a week, read through this comprehensive list of tips as review and reinforcement. Use these mnemonics (memory devices) to claim new words and boost your lexicon and strengthen your working vocabulary!

Try to make up your own memory clues for words in this book (in addition to other new words you come across) that you find particularly challenging. Add these tips, and your own, to index cards, or keep a notebook of vocabulary tips. You can color code index cards in various ways. For example, green cards for positive connotation words; red cards for negative feel words. Or you can color code your flash cards by part of speech: one color for verbs, one color for adjectives, a different color for people, and so on.

---

## LESSON 1

**accustomed**
To connect to this vocabulary word, focus in on the basic word built into it: *custom*. Just as a custom is an aspect of life that people are used to, so **accustomed** means feeling familiar with or habituated to something or someone.

**bristled**
Picture the *bristle*s of a hairbrush. They are pointy, coarse, and sharp to the touch.
Connect these tangible feelings to the emotions behind the verb *bristled*: bitterness, coarseness, sometimes even fear.

**embittered**
Focus on the basic word built into this word: *bitter.* Knowledge of this stem word will help you remember the meaning of **embittered**: "feeling bitter, resentful, or disillusioned."

**frailness**
Think *frail*. Now link *frail* to a mental picture of a thin, rickety, wooden *rail* that is ramshackle, unsteady, and about to fall down. This visual mnemonic device will help you to remember that frail pertains to people or things that are weak, unsteady, or debilitated to some extent or another.

## LESSON 2

### primordial
Split this word into two parts: *prim* and *ord*. Expand these parts to create the phrase, "primitive order." Creatively cutting a word into its parts is a great way to recall and harness its meaning.

### unison
The prefix *uni-* means "one" or "singular." Consider this prefix as it is used in *uni*lateral, *uni*versal, *uni*corn, *uni*cycle, and *uni*cellular. When people are singing in unison, they are singing as if they shared one voice.

## LESSON 3

### concoct
Consider the prefix *con-* (*con-* means "with, together") in words such as *concordance, congregate, convene,* and *connect.* Also, let concoct and combine connect in your mind as viable synonyms. Both have two syllables and start with *co-*, which is another prefix meaning "together."

### disheartens
The prefix *dis-* has a negative, reversing force. Depending on the word in which it appears, *dis-* can also mean "away from" or "against." Recall the use of *dis-* in these words: *disallow, disembark, disappear, disbelieving, dislike, disagree, disapprove, disregard,* and so forth. If someone **disheartens** your dream of starting a business, he or she "works against" or "takes away" your ambitious, entrepreneurial heart or spirit.

### introspective
Split this word into two parts: *intro* and *spect*. As a prefix, *intro-* means "within" and "inwardly." As a root word, *spect* has to do with seeing, as in in*spect*, *spect*acles, *spect*ator, and circum*spect*. Breaking down a word into its parts is a great way to remember its meaning.

### lush
Visualize in your mind's eye a supersized bright green "lush bush." Actively picture this **lush** bush brimming with large, green healthy leaves! Recite this tongue-twisting chant to secure this word's meaning: "Lush bush! Lush bush! Lush bush!"

## LESSON 4

### array

Rhyming clues can be particularly effective. *Array* and *display* rhyme. Let these sentences, which incorporate *array* and *display*, help you solidify this word's definition. Remember, an **array** is a large collection or group of things that relate to each other...

The jewelry party hostess will now *display* an eye-catching *array* of bedazzled earrings.

Jack is happy to *display* his *array* of sports collectibles and baseball caps.

Excited to *display* his *array* of Italian desserts, the pastry chef assembles a Viennese table brimming with cannoli, éclairs, and rainbow cookies.

### breadth

Ciabatta rolls, French baguettes, Italian bread, challah, rye, wheat, pumpernickel, sourdough....Think about the expansive variety of bread there is in the world. Now let *bread*, found in *bread*th, remind you that **breadth** pertains to the far-reaching range of something.

### dissonance

The prefix *dis-* means "against" or "without." Consider this prefix in words such as *disconnected, disagreement, discouraged,* and *disjointed. Sonic* means pertaining to sound. Recall how dolphins use sonic communication to call to and locate one another in the water. Put the word parts together and you get something like "against sound," another way of saying "without harmony."

## LESSON 5

### discontent

*Dis-* is a negative-indicating prefix. Depending on the word in which it appears, *dis-* can mean "against" or "not." Consider this prefix as used in *disavow, disrespect, disagree, disrepair,* and *disappear*. So, individuals who are **discontent** are *not* feeling content, satisfied, or happy.

## penned

If a wrestler is "pinned down" on the mat in one of his fighting matches then, in a sense, his opponent has our wrestler "confined or controlled," which is a solid definition for **penned**. Again, to make new vocabulary words your own, creatively link familiar and similar sounding words to your new vocabulary words.

## tinged

If one's actions leave one feeling "tinged with guilt," then these emotions are, in a sense, tinted (colored, painted) with guilt. Tinted windows on a sports car are highlighted or aesthetically touched up with a smoky gray shade. **Tinged** and *tinted* look and sound similar, so you can use your familiarity with *tinted* to connect you to the meaning of **tinged**.

---

# LESSON 6

## circumscribed

Let *circum-* reminded you of *circum*ference, the length of the line around a circle. Consider the use of this prefix in additional words such as *circum*vent, *circum*navigate, and *circum*locution. Connect this prefix to *scribe*, which means "a writer or copier of text." Knowledge of these stem words will help you piece together and recall this word's meaning more easily.

## legitimate

Let the *leg-* at the beginning of this word remind you of the word *leg*al, which is a viable synonym in many contexts of this word's use; for example, legitimate business affairs, legitimate claims to property, and legitimate concerns about someone's motives. Legitimate grounds for suing a company, for example, are those that are lawful and right; in other words, they relate to that which is legally sound and in compliance with the law.

## perquisite

Link this lengthy word to its short and sweet definition: *perk*. Simply swap out the *q* for a *k* and you've got this simple definition! Just to review, a *perk* is a bonus, an extra, or a benefit that one receives through employment or some other affiliation. A *perk* is always a plus!

**populace**
Let the whole word remind you of _population_. In Latin, _populous_ refers to population. Consider how anything _popular_ tends to be well-liked and embraced by the majority of the population.

---

## LESSON 7

**credulity**
_Cred-_ means "believe." Consider the meaning of this prefix as used in _creed, credo, credit, credence, incredible_, and _incredulous_. Individuals who are known for their **credulity**, tend to believe most of what they hear. To an extent, these people can be considered gullible.

**disavows**
The prefix _dis-_ indicates "negation, a lacking of, or a reversal." He who **disavows** his statements rescinds or takes back what he has said. In a sense, he is "reversing" his words. Consider the use of _dis-_ in these words: _disconnect, disembark, dissimilar, disengage, distrust,_ and _disrespect_.

**sacrilegious**
The final three syllables of this word sound like _religious_. Use this sound-alike clue to connect you to the meaning of this word: "irreverent, heretical, blasphemous."

**spawn**
Did you know that another name for shrimp is _prawn_? Prawns come in several varieties, such as king prawns and tiger prawns. Calling all auditory and visual learners: Allow yourselves to hear and see the word _prawn_ within **spawn**. Think of _prawns spawn_ing in the ocean waters. The similar look and sound of these words will help you recall the meaning of **spawn**.

---

## LESSON 8

**durable**
Consider how the word root _dura_ suggests the idea of "long lasting" in words you may know such as en_dura_nce, _dura_tion, and en_dure_. Have you heard of Duraflame® fire logs or Duracell batteries? The _dura-_ prefix accentuates the long-lasting flames, which are perfect for a campfire or

roasting pit. Likewise, *dura-* calls attention to the long-lasting power of the batteries.

## onus

Imagine two buddies talking:

> "Hey, Buddy, the **onus** is *on us* to get this job done."

> "Yep, I know. I feel the **onus** on our shoulders."

> "Think positive! If we take seriously this **onus**, we are more likely to receive that b*onus*!"

## streamlined

Picture a stream running through a forest. If you're like most, you probably picture a meandering pathway of water with lots of ins and outs, bends and curves. Now imagine that same stream straightened out into a simple *line*. The stream has been **streamlined** or simplified in your mind's eye! Use this visual memory clue to cement the meaning of this word in your memory.

---

# LESSON 9

## barren

Think *bare* (empty, vacant, blank, lacking) when you read and hear *barren*. A field "bare" of corn and wheat is a barren field. A woman who is **barren** cannot have children. An author who cannot think of topics to write about finds himself **barren** of ideas and inspiration.

## inordinate

The prefix *in-* means "not." So, simply break down *inordinate* to mean "not ordinary." For example, an **inordinate** number of required volunteer hours or an **inordinate** price for a pair of boots is beyond reason, immoderate, or excessive. Knowledge of this prefix and stem word will help you piece together and recall this word's meaning.

---

# LESSON 10

## courtiers

Let *court*, which is built in to this word, remind you of attendants to the royal *court,* where **courtiers** are apt (likely) to be found.

**erroneous**
Let the first four letters lead you to picture a word you undoubtedly know: *error*. **Erroneous** research findings are faulty because they contain *error*. Likewise, **erroneous** conclusions can be misleading, murky, or downright false.

**façade**
To review, a **façade** is a deceptive or false appearance. Think of the human <u>fac</u>e as a type of mask or **<u>fac</u>ade**, a false cover or exterior. Some individuals conceal their emotions of sadness or desperation behind a cheerful smile. Likewise, some conceal their insecurities behind other facial expressions, such as a grimace, scowl, frown, or snarl. For example, her congenial conversation and pleasant face are merely a **façade** for the deception that lurks within.

**ravages**
Link this word to a rhyming word that you know, *savages*. Now picture a vivid scene in which *savages* are the cause of sweeping **ravages** (destruction, ruin, fire …) experienced by the ransacked village!

**simulation**
Let *sim* lead you to the word <u>sim</u>ilar. A **simulation** creates a situation or effect that feels *similar* to the actual thing. At the Atlantis Marine World aquarium in Riverhead, Long Island, New York, there is a *simulated* submarine ride that is a big attraction for guests. Likewise, St. Luke's feast offers a towering and spine-tingling ride *simulating* bungee jumping!

---

# LESSON 11

**inherently**

Link this word to a word you likely already know from biology class: *inherited*. Think of the term, "inherited traits." Note these viable synonyms that all happen to start with *in-*: intrinsically, innately, and instinctively.

**overtly**
Slant rhyme **overtly** with *openly*. People who **overtly** express their emotions do so openly and demonstratively. Another tip for remembering this word is to notice that *overt* and *covert* are antonyms. *Covert* means "hidden." (Think "covered.")

## LESSON 12

### alienation

Imagine how an alien would feel if he found himself sitting among you and your classmates in AP Bio or among you and your friends in Period 7 lunch! He would feel out of place or out of his comfort zone. (Is he more comfortable on Mars?) Now, link this visual story to the definition of **alienation**, which is "an uncomfortable feeling of distance or estrangement."

### memoirs

Let the sound and look of the word **memoirs** remind you of *memories*. To a great extent, memoir writers rely on their *memories* for their creative, narrative material.

### visionary

Focus on *vision* when you encounter the word **visionary**. Possessing some degree of extrasensory perception, a **visionary**, to an arguable extent, can *envision* or see aspects of the future.

## LESSON 13

### bemoans

If Margo *moans* about how her soufflé collapsed, then she is expressing sadness about something. If your dog *moans* in his sleep, you can imagine he is dreaming about his doggie biscuit treats being depleted.

### disconcerting

People who are in *concert* with one another are in harmonious agreement. Given that the prefix *dis-* means "against," it makes sense that **disconcerting** means "upsetting or lacking in harmony." *Dis-* is also used in *disagreeable, disappearance, dissonance,* and *disassemble.*

### rendition

In a sense, this word has one of its definitions built in: "edition." A new edition of a song, for example, can come out as a remix, as a dance-tech version, or as an amalgam (blend) of a few top songs.

# LESSON 14

**bog**
Picture this wet, muddy scene: rolling over and splashing around, the *hog* (adult male pig) is delightfully cooling himself off in the chilly *bog*!

**lax**
Think re*lax*ed. Or picture a re*lax*ed **lax** coach who is easygoing and jovial, whether or not his team wins the Eastern Seaboard Lacrosse Tournament!

**retrospection**
The word roots *spic* and *spec* pertain to seeing and looking, as used in in*spec*t, *spec*tacle, or *spec*tate. The prefix *retro-* means prior or early. Piece these word parts together to get a working definition of **retrospection**: "seeing the prior picture." Just as hindsight is twenty-twenty, so oftentimes **retrospection** is twenty-twenty, as well.

# LESSON 15

**premier**
The commonly used prefix *pre-* means "before" and sometimes can be used to mean "first," "prior," "preliminary," or "early." Think of this prefix's usage in words such as *pre*amble, *pre*school, *pre*arranged, *pre*maturity, and *pre*cooked. So the *pre*mier showing of the play is the first in line, the first performance of its kind.

**punctuate**
Think about how punctuation marks such as the question mark (?) and the exclamation point (!) stress or accentuate the tone and meaning of a sentence.

# LESSON 16

**longevity**
To harness the meaning of this word in a nutshell, think "long life." As you recall, **longevity** refers to the life span of a person or animal as well as the span of one's career.

**prowess**
Scramble the letters in **prowess** to get *powers*! As we can think of *powers* as great skills and abilities, the word *powers* provides a helpful link to the meaning of **prowess**.

**subjective**
A *subject* is the person being written about, spoken about, or referred to. For example, the subject of a biography might be Eleanor Roosevelt or Lance Armstrong. Given that a subject is an individual, think of how **subjective** points of view are those based on an individual subject's opinions and points of view.

---

## LESSON 17

**illuminant**
Picture a beautiful luminary, such as white bags filled with candles lining the walkway to a home, welcoming you to a soirée (an evening get-together). Envision lily-shaped luminaries floating in a backyard pool in the evening, giving off enough light to toast s'mores in a fire pit.

**opus**
A simple definition for **opus** is a *work*, as in a work of art. Usually, an *opus* refers to a musical work or composition. Simply connect this four-letter definition (w-o-r-k) with the four-letter vocabulary word, o-p-u-s. As easy as 1-2-3-4.

---

## LESSON 18

**terrestrial**
The word root *terra* relates to and signifies "dry land, earth, soil, and the ground." Consider its use in common words such as *terrain, territory,* and *terra-cotta.*

**vaporizes**
Visualize how the Star Trek characters **vaporize** as they stand on their platform and travel from one place to another. In this scientific world, their bodies turn to *vapor* (steam, mist) as they are transported to a new location.

# LESSON 19

**colleagues**
Picture the word *colleges* embedded within this word. Think of one's **colleagues** at college being his classmates and peers.

**extract**
Let the prefix ex- (which means "out," "out of," and "from") remind you that **extract** means to take something out, usually by force. Consider the appearance of ex- in *expunge, expel,* and *expurgate.*

# LESSON 20

**minuscule**
**Minuscule** derives from the word *minus*, to make smaller. As a prefix, *min-* means "little" or "small." Think of its usage in *minute, minor, miniature, minicomputer*, and *miniskirt*. Granules of salt are **minuscule** in size compared to colored sprinkles.

**submersible**
Link this word to *submarine*. Also note that the prefix *sub-* means "under" or "below." Think of *subway, subatomic*, and *subterranean* ("below the earth's surface"). **Submersibles** are vehicles, vessels, crafts, or other objects that can function under water without sustaining damage.

# LESSON 21

**preceding**
Let the prefix *pre-* (which means "first," "before," or "early") remind you that **preceding** refers to that which comes first or before. Notice that *pre-* is used in the following words: *premature, preamble, prequalify.*

**relevant**
Link *related* to **relevant**. Both words have three syllables, and start with the same three letters. Challenge yourself to learn these upper level synonyms for relevant: *germane* and *pertinent.*

## LESSON 22

### acute
In mathematics, consider how acute angles (less than 90 degrees), relative to obtuse angles (more than 90 degrees), form more pointed angles and, therefore, have *sharper* points. Link this geometry definition to the definition of **acute** as "*sharp*-minded, keen, perceptive."

### alpha
In the Greek alphabet, **alpha** is the first letter. Accordingly, let **alpha** remind you of "first," "beginning," "leading," and "highest in rank."

### vitality
In Latin, *vita* means "life." *Vi-* and *viva-* are also prefixes and words stems that indicate "life." Consider these root words' use in words and phrases such as: *vi*tamin, *vi*tal, *vi*gor, *viva*cious, con*vivi*al, and curriculum *vitae*.

## LESSON 23

### agronomist
*Agro-* is derived from the French and Greek and means "pertaining to fields and soil." Think of its use in words and phrases such as *agriculture, agrarian,* and *agro-industrial.*

### recounted
Did you know that a *raconteur* is a storyteller? Let *raconteur* cue you into the meaning of the verb, **recount** ("to tell a story, to narrate"). For auditory and visual learners, this mnemonic device can be effective, as *raconteur* and *recount* look and sound similar.

## LESSON 24

### coalition
The popular prefix, *co-,* means "with" or "together." Consider the use of *co-* in words such as community, copilot, cohabitate, committee, and coalesce. Connect this prefix meaning to the meaning of the **coalition**: a group working "together," or allied with each other.

**exemplifies**

Allow the sound and sight of this word to remind you of the word *example*. If Mother **exemplifies** patience, then her manner and conduct serve as a leading *example* of patience. The Statue of Liberty **exemplifies** freedom.

**orient**

Think of the **Orient** as a geographical location on the map. Link this understanding to the meaning of **orient** that has to do with positioning one thing in relation to other things. Think of college *orient*ation as a time during which freshman **orient** themselves to the new surroundings of their campus, dormitories, and facilities.

---

## LESSON 25

**sojourner**

See the word *journey* within **so*journe*r**. This visual mnemonic clue can help you remember that a **sojourner** is one who travels or takes a *journey*.

**staggering**

A *stag* is a male deer. Some adult stags can weigh close to three hundred pounds. Now that is a **staggering** weight! Recall that **staggering** means "tending to astonish or fascinate." Here's an alliterative picture clue: Stately and strapping, the **staggering** stag strolled stoically.

**undaunted**

Think of *unhaunted* (a made-up word) as a way of remembering the meaning of this word. "**Undaunted** (*unhaunted*), Leo entered the undulating doorway of the haunted house."

# Answer Key

## LESSON 1
**Matching**
1. C    2. D    3. E    4. A    5. B

**Words in Context**
1. C    2. C    3. C    4. I    5. C

## LESSON 2
**Matching**
1. C    2. E    3. A    4. F    5. B

**Words in Context**
1. I    2. C    3. C    4. I    5. I

## LESSON 3
**Matching**
1. E    2. C    3. G    4. F    5. D

**Words in Context**
1. I    2. C    3. C    4. C    5. C

## LESSON 4
**Matching**
1. F    2. D    3. E    4. G    5. B

**Words in Context**
1. C    2. C    3. C    4. C    5. C

## LESSON 5

**Matching**
1. C      2. G      3. E      4. A      5. D

**Words in Context**
1. C      2. C      3. C      4. C      5. I

## LESSON 6

**Matching**
1. C      2. E      3. G      4. B      5. F

**Words in Context**
1. I      2. C      3. I      4. C      5. C

## LESSON 7

**Matching**
1. F      2. G      3. D      4. E      5. B

**Words in Context**
1. I      2. C      3. C      4. C      5. C

## LESSON 8

**Matching**
1. C      2. D      3. A      4. F      5. E

**Words in Context**
1. C      2. I      3. I      4. C      5. C

## LESSON 9

**Matching**

1. D    2. C    3. A    4. G    5. E

**Words in Context**

1. I    2. C    3. C    4. C    5. C

## LESSON 10

**Matching**

1. A    2. E    3. G    4. B    5. C

**Words in Context**

1. I    2. I    3. C    4. C    5. C

## LESSON 11

**Matching**

1. B    2. D    3. A    4. G    5. E

**Words in Context**

1. I    2. I    3. C    4. C    5. I

## LESSON 12

**Matching**

1. A    2. C    3. G    4. E    5. B

**Words in Context**

1. I    2. I    3. I    4. C    5. C

## LESSON 13

**Matching**
1. A       2. C       3. D       4. G       5. E

**Words in Context**
1. C       2. C       3. C       4. I       5. C

## LESSON 14

**Matching**
1. G       2. E       3. B       4. D       5. A

**Words in Context**
1. C       2. C       3. I       4. C       5. C

## LESSON 15

**Matching**
1. E       2. B       3. D       4. A       5. F

**Words in Context**
1. C       2. C       3. C       4. C       5. I

## LESSON 16

**Matching**
1. B       2. C       3. G       4. D       5. E

**Words in Context**
1. C       2. C       3. C       4. I       5. C

## LESSON 17
**Matching**
1. E    2. C    3. G    4. A    5. B

**Words in Context**
1. C    2. C    3. I    4. I    5. C

## LESSON 18
**Matching**
1. C    2. F    3. D    4. E    5. A

**Words in Context**
1. I    2. C    3. C    4. C    5. C

## LESSON 19
**Matching**
1. D    2. G    3. C    4. A    5. B

**Words in Context**
1. C    2. C    3. C    4. C    5. C

## LESSON 20
**Matching**
1. C    2. A    3. D    4. B    5. F

**Words in Context**
1. C    2. C    3. I    4. I    5. C

## LESSON 21

**Matching**

1. D     2. G     3. C     4. B     5. A

**Words in Context**

1. C     2. C     3. C     4. C     5. I

## LESSON 22

**Matching**

1. C     2. A     3. F     4. E     5. B

**Words in Context**

1. C     2. C     3. C     4. C     5. C

## LESSON 23

**Matching**

1. G     2. E     3. C     4. B     5. A

**Words in Context**

1. C     2. I     3. I     4. C     5. C

## LESSON 24

**Matching**

1. B     2. A     3. E     4. G     5. C

**Words in Context**

1. C     2. I     3. C     4. C     5. C

## LESSON 25

**Matching**

1. A      2. F      3. D      4. E      5. C

**Words in Context**

1. C      2. C      3. I      4. C      5. C

# Index of
# ACT Vocabulary Words

These are the key words taken from each lesson. Lessons in which the vocabulary words appear are indicated by the numeral.

Scope, 12
Sentiments, 7
Septillion, 19
Serenity, 3
Simulation, 10
Sojourner, 25
Sovereign, 11
Spawned, 7
Specimen, 19
Speculate, 4
Staggering, 25
Stance, 20
Stifle, 23
Streamlined, 8
Subjective, 16
Submersibles, 20
Subsequently, 23
Succession, 18
Sulky, 5

Supplement, 13
Tableau, 10
Tendrilous, 20
Terrestrial, 18
Tinged, 5
Uncannily, 18
Undaunted, 25
Unison, 2
Unparalleled, 12
Unsolicited, 23
Unsuspecting, 22
Utility, 9
Vaporizes, 18
Visionary, 12
Vital, 19
Vitality, 22
Voluptuous, 2
Vulnerability, 2
Whet, 25

# Index of Words from Test Takers' Anecdotes

Test takers' anecdotes precede every lesson in this book. Anecdotes give you glimpses into test takers' experiences as they work through the verbal portions of the ACT exam. Using specific examples, based on real test takers' experiences, the purpose of these anecdotes is to illustrate how rich and diverse with upper level vocabulary that the ACT verbal passages truly are.

For the particular context in which a word was used, refer to the example within the indicated lesson. For example, in Lesson 22, **concrete** is used as an adjective, not as a noun. Likewise, in that same lesson, **contract** is used as a verb, not as a noun. Similarly, **clearing** (Lesson 23) would have been a very accessible word if, as an action verb, it had to do with "clearing the dinner table" or "clearing a path at the front door." In context, however, **clearing** was used as a noun meaning, "a clear and unobstructed space," such as one might encounter on the side of a rural road.

As further evidenced by the substantial alphabetical listing of words that follows, taking the ACT English and Reading Test involves a reading experience that is infused with a rich vocabulary. As you tackled the reading passages on the test, not all of the words in the list that follows will present obstacles for you. Still, take note of the broad array of vocabulary that was included on just the several practice tests surveyed to put this list together. The more words you master, the better your reading comprehension, and the higher you will score.

**Exercise 1:** Quiz yourself or ask someone to quiz you on your understanding of a given word. Then go to the test-takers' anecdotes to see if your definition matches up with the word as used in context.

**Exercise 2:** Using accents of color, make flashcards for the words that have new or unfamiliar definitions for you. Consider your flashcards your personalized "short list" of words to solidify.